THE JOURNEY OF
100 HIDDEN HEARTS

A Spiritual Path to Your Hidden Heart

DR JOHN MCSWINEY

By Dr John McSwiney

The Fight against 'Good As' Labor Men. *The Australian Labor Party and the Federal Platform 1901-1910*

The Platform Becomes Law. *The Australian Labor Party and the Federal Platform 1910-1916*

Scullin and the Great Depression. *The Australian Labor Party and the Federal Platform 1929-1931*

Curtin, Labor and Total War. *The Australian Labor Party and the Federal Platform 1940-1945*

Chifley and Postwar Reconstruction. *The Australian Labor Party and the Federal Platform 1945-1949*

" HAVE THE COURAGE TO FOLLOW
YOUR HEART AND INTUITION.
THEY SOMEHOW KNOW WHAT
YOU WANT TO BECOME "

Steve Jobs

A catalogue record for this work is available from the National Library of Australia

https://www.drjohnmcswiney.com
McSwiney, John (author)
The Journey of 100 Hidden Hearts: A Spiritual Path to Your Hidden Heart
ISBN 978-1-922722-31-7
SELF HELP
LIFE TRANSFORMATION

Typeset Whitman 11/16
Cover and book design by Green Hill Publishing

This Book is dedicated to the loving memory of my brother Daniel who was tragically taken from this world on 5 August 1989 only three months after his 20th birthday.

Daniel's beautiful heart was there for the world to see and a chosen few of us got to experience it; and we are better for it. His spirit lives on and he will be remembered forever by all who knew and loved him.

John xox

CONTENTS

X

"There is no greater gift you can giver or receive than to honour your calling. It is why you were born and how you become most truly alive"
OPRAH WINFREY

THE JOURNEY OF 100 HIDDEN HEARTS - GOAL AND MISSION

My goal is for 1 million people to read this Book and use it to connect with their hearts and transform their lives.

My mission is to connect every person with their hearts: it is a legacy gift.

The Journey of 100 Hidden Hearts is a part of that goal and mission because I want people to live empowered heart centered lives. Your Hidden Heart is unique to you and defines your very essence. It is evolving, changing and growing every year just as you evolve, change and grow. It reflects who you are and can be captured to help you live into your best life.

My journey is to ensure this Book is being read, enjoyed and felt by millions (and in time, Billions) of people, like yourself, all over the world. Copies of this Book will be gifted and donated each year to schools, community groups, organisations, and individuals in need of encouragement, inspiration, guidance, and compassion.

In addition to gifting copies of the Book every year I will also be donating 5% of the royalties from each copy of this Book that is sold to nonprofit charities including The Hearting the World Foundation to promote the Hidden Heart message.

I want you to connect with your heart, so that you can start to live an empowered and compassionate heart centered life one day, one month and one (Hidden Heart) year at a time.

Thankyou so much for your heartfelt love and support, it is greatly appreciated.

"My mission in life is not merely to survive, but to thrive; and to do so with some passion, some humor, and some style"
MAYA ANGELOU

"The journey of a thousand miles begins with a single step"
LAO TZU

A HEARTING INVITATION FOR YOU TO JOIN THE ONLINE COMMUNITY FOR *THE JOURNEY OF 100 HIDDEN HEARTS*

You are now part of a worldwide community who are on a journey of discovery inwards. It is a journey that you take alone but in communion with like hearted souls who want to make a positive contribution to the world and leave a legacy of compassion, joy and love for future generations.

I have set up a Facebook page called *The Journey of 100 Hidden Hearts* so jump on your Facebook and join me and your fellow Hidden Heart buddies. It is a safe space where you can come together to share your heart journeys and how you are using your hidden heart marbles to live into your best lives for yourself and those around you.

Your life is an amazing journey and it is important that you join with people who are on the same spiritual path as you. You have your own unique spiritual energy and it is important to fee into it and let it guide you. When you connect with your heart your frequency and vibration resonate at a higher level and you attract fellow souls at this elevated plane.

I invite you to feel into your heart and connect with the true you. The You you were always destined to be. When you do this you will feel your life start to change in ways you never imagined.

Your heart knows your true path all you need to do is connect with it and let it lead you to your Hidden Heart.

"Maybe the journey isn't so much about becoming anything. Maybe it's about unbecoming everything that isn't really you so you can be who you were meant to be in the first place"
UNKNOWN

WHY HAS *THE JOURNEY OF 100 HIDDEN HEARTS* COME ACROSS YOUR PATH?

You are reading this Book because the Universe has brought you here right now for the purpose of making a choice.

The choice to continue on your current path or to decide whether to move forward with your heart towards your destiny and live into your best life with heartfelt compassion for yourself and others.

I invite you to consider a personal challenge from me to you: it is a challenge that will transform your life. Read this Book in its entirety and then implement all the heart learnings, Heart Whispers and Heart Trysts and see what happens: or not. The choice is yours!

I also invite you to be courageous and feel into your heart and honestly take your hearts pulse *(your hearts true beat)* and ask yourself:

- How are you truly feeling about your life, health and wellbeing, work and career, physical environment, fun and recreation, personal growth, relationships and romance, financial security and family and friends?
- What is a part of your life now that does not serve you?

The conscious awareness of your current life situation is not enough. You must also take action which you are genuinely committed to. There are no half measures in your journey of life because half measures get you to where you are right now and how is that working out for you?

Compassionate action is the key to connecting with your heart and then finding your Hidden Heart and living into your best life. I invite you to consider the proposition that simply being conscious that you need to take action is only part of the equation.

You also genuinely need to step up, be fully present and make positive heartfelt changes to your current life.

Congratulations! If you are reading this then you have already started taking action and can start to truly feel into your heart; acknowledge that you are where you need to be and are doing what you need to do right in this moment.

It is your choice now whether you will journey into your heart space and I truly hope that you continue because the affects on you and your world will be deep and profound.

You may have believed that you have had the power to live your life any way you wanted and your head and your ego has convinced you that this is indeed the case. However, emotional wounds, trauma, pain, fear, rejection, abandonment, and a myriad of other life impacting events have caused you to close your heart and disconnect from it.

Remember that your life changes the moment you decide to take heartfelt action. So, close your eyes, put your hand on your heart, listen to your breathing and feel your heart. Ask it:

What does your heart truly want?

What does your heart truly desire?

What does your heart truly connect with?

Your heart knows exactly what you need and you will feel it!

HEARTING EXERCISE

I invite you now to get a pen and draw a line down the middle of a page. Now write down the last eleven times you truly felt into your heart and acted out of

XVI *"Self-compassion is nurturing your-self with all the kindness and love you would shower on someone you cherish"*
DEBRA L. REBLE

compassion for yourself and for others. Write two headings, 'yourself', and 'others' at the top of the page! Go on, find a pen and paper and write them down: just eleven.

Now put a time and date next to them. When did they actually occur? Interesting isn't it? I would be amazed if the column headed 'yourself' has more actions in it than 'others'.

Now keep that paper with you over the next 24 hours and every time you act with compassion for yourself write it down and the time you did it. At the end of the day look at the list. What does it look like? What does it feel like to look at it? Are you surprised? Excited? Angry? Sad? Confused?

Self-compassion and self-love are the first steps in helping you reconnect with your own heart. People have the ability to show empathy and compassion for others and that is beautiful, however they find it difficult and, in a lot of cases, almost impossible to genuinely reach into their own hearts and show themselves compassion. The internal interaction most people have with themselves is negative and self-destructive. This just keeps their heart closed off and locked away and that is tragic!

Now imagine your life and what you could do if you started to think and feel differently and create new positive connections with yourself and your heart.

It will change your life in every way and provide you with a new connection with your heart that will empower you to live the life you were always destined to.

Connect with your Heart and Live into your best life today!

HOW TO USE THIS BOOK TO CONNECT WITH YOUR HIDDEN HEART

I invite you to feel into your heart and get yourself a special journal either electronic or hardcopy. This will help you take note of your hearting exercises, hearting questions, heart activation exercises, and Hidden Heart Learnings in the Book as well as noting every time you use one of your precious Hidden Heart life marbles. It will become a compendium of your life and dreams to compliment everything you will do in this Book.

A book like this is unique in that there are many ways to approach it because it is not really a straight linear, cover to cover experience. I have felt into it and there are three distinct paths that you can take with it, and each will take you where you need to go, for where you are in your life right now.

PATH 1: THE RANDOM INTUITIVE PATH – I invite you to feel into your heart and let it guide you to where it truly wants and desires to be. What is your heart connecting with at a particular time that it wants you to know and experience? You literally pick up the Book and ask your heart to guide you into it. It does not get any simpler, yet very intuitive as that.

PATH 2: THE SEQUENTIAL PATH – There is a basic structure in the Sequential path, and it will take you through the Book in an orderly manner.

Step 1 – Your 100 Hidden Hearts

Go to Part VI and have a quick look at your 100 Hidden Hearts and the page that corresponds with your age. This page represents your spiritual jar of life marbles from birth to 100. I invite you to read through your page and feel into the enormity of your life clock and the time you have already used, as well as the time you have left if you live to 100. It is a sobering exercise for a lot of people. Do you truly feel you have been living into your best life?

Take a moment and feel into your heart and ask it what it truly wants and desires for you to connect with it. Remember that every moment that passes is time you will not have again. So, how do you want to spend the rest of your life?

Step 2 – The Genesis of The Hidden Heart Journey

Go to Part I and read the Genesis of The Hidden Heart Journey and discover a little bit about the author and why this Book was written and why you are reading it right now.

There are no coincidences and as you allow yourself to feel into your heart as you read Part I you will feel your hearts pull to be released and fully embraced within you. You will have a choice, connect with your heart, or keep living into your life how you always have. It's your time now to step up and be who you were always created to be.

Step 3 – Be courageous and connect with the true You

Go to Part II and commence the next steps in your journey. Take your time and move through your heart clock, practice your hidden heart breathing, and complete your Heart Connection Oath.

I invite you to make it official that you value yourself enough to be compassionate towards you as a human becoming, complete the hearting questions and enjoy your introduction to your first heart activation exercises with your Heart Trysts and Heart Whispers they will change your life.

Step 4 – Time to Connect with Your Hidden Heart

Go to Part III – The Metaphysical Framework to Connect with Your Hidden Heart and introduce yourself to your Hidden Heart Diamond and feel into and discover an exciting and empowering part of your journey to connect with your heart.

I invite you to feel into your heart and connect with Source, your inner child, your heart, and your life purpose; when you do this you will feel into and connect with your Hidden Heart. As you discover more about connecting with your Hidden Heart Diamond you will develop skills and use tools to identify and lessen the impact of your Ego in all areas of your life.

In the process of journeying inward you will also develop practices and understandings about connecting at a deep level in critical areas of your life that have always been a part of you but have been cloaked and ignored for years and even decades. Your journey of self-discovery will reveal your heart and open your life in ways you have never imagined.

XX

"You cannot swim for new horizons until you have courage to lose sight of the shore"
WILLIAM FAULKNER

"Only when brave enough to explore the darkness will we discover the infinite power of our light"
BRENE BROWN

Step 5 – Your Hidden Heart Diamond

Your Hidden Heart Diamond and your journey of connection is a key part of constructing your relationship with yourself. To strengthen and expand your transformation go to Part IV and Part V and fully immerse yourself in all the Hidden Heart Learnings and Exceptional Hearting Self-care.

In these sections there are a number of learnings and exercises that you are strongly encouraged to complete. These exercises have been designed to guide you in your own journey of self-discovery, personal empowerment, transformation and connection to your heart.

They have been designed so that you have templates to use for the rest of your life. Your values, shadow values, goals, dreams and aspirations can change many times over your life. These heart learnings and hearting exercises will help you be more creative, courageous, and compassionate in your journey to find your own path to wisdom and your Hidden Heart. So take your time and connect with your heart in all that you do.

PATH 3: THE HEART TRANSFORMATION SERIES PATH

This path is a life journey that is structured to take you on a deep heart connection adventure. It is comprised of a four part program reflective of your Hidden Heart Diamond, and the four chambers of your heart:

- Heart Connection
- Heart Awakening
- Heart Expansion
- Heart Amplification

I invite you to use the following structure and the Table of Contents to guide you to the relevant section. I am gifting you a 6-month program that will connect, awaken, expand, and amplify your relationship with your heart and transform your life. You will undertake and complete one session every week, or not, the choice is always Yours!

PART I – HEART CONNECTION PROGRAM

Session 1 – Heart Connection Program Introduction

- Balanced Heart Breathing
- Heart Connection Oath
- Program Expectations
- Heart Whispers
- Heart Trysts
- Heartbeat Buddies
- 30-day Heart Connection Life Challenges

Session 2 – Hidden Heart Diamond

- Source
- Inner Child
- Heart (Compassionate Mind)
- Life Purpose
- Ego
- Hidden Heart

Session 3 – Hidden Heart Diamond – Hearting your Ego

- Your Ego
- Guiding your Ego
- Tiny Monkey to Killer King Kong
- Spiritual Ego Identification

Session 4 – Hidden Heart Diamond – Hearting your Inner Child

- Inner Child Woundings
- Reconnecting and Reparenting your Inner Child

- Questions and Exercises to Reconnect with your Inner Child

Session 5 – Heart Connection Celebration
- Recap
- Learnings
- Moving forward

PART II – HEART AWAKENING PROGRAM – STRUCTURE

Session 1 – Hidden Heart Diamond – Source
- Balanced Heart Breathing; Heart Awakening Oath; Program Expectations; Heart Whispers; Heart Trysts; Heartbeat Buddies; Hidden Heart Diamond; 30-day Heart Awakening Life Challenges
- Spiritual Darkness and Shadow
- How to connect to Source
- Spiritual Synchronicities and Signs
- Source connection meditation
- Your Senses and Your Sixth Sense
- Crown and Third Eye Chakra
- Developing Your Intuition
- The Four Clairs

Session 2 – Hidden Heart Diamond – Heart (Compassionate Mind)
- What is the scientific definition of your heart?
- Fun facts about your heart
- What is the metaphysical and spiritual definition of your heart?
- What is the *m*Braining perspective of your heart?
- Heart based language (Idioms and Sayings)
- Heart as your fourth chakra
- Fourth chakra healing foods and crystals

- Your own gratitude practices
- What brings you joy?
- What are your top joys?

Session 4 – Hidden Heart Years
- Your 100 Hidden Hearts
- Your life in a jar of marbles
- Your Hidden Heartlines
- Your Hidden Heart Seven Year Life Review

Session 5 – Heart Expansion Celebration
- Recap
- Learnings
- Moving forward

PART IV – HEART AMPLIFICATION PROGRAM

Session 1 – Heart Existence Mirror –
Health and Wellbeing
- Balanced Heart Breathing; Heart Amplification Oath; Program Expectations; Heart Whispers; Heart Trysts; Heartbeat Buddies; Hidden Heart Diamond; 90-day Heart Amplification Life Challenges
- Physical fitness; nutrition; sleep; self-care; medical issues
- Heart Existence Mirror Ranking
- Heart Existence Questions and Actions

Session 2 – Heart Existence Mirror –
Work and Career
- Work hours; career direction and purpose; performance; environment; colleagues
- Heart Existence Mirror Ranking
- Heart Existence Questions and Actions

Session 8 – Heart Existence Mirror – Family and Friends

- Family; friends; community
- Heart Existence Mirror Ranking
- Heart Existence Questions and Actions

Session 9 – Future Heart Map

- What is your future heart map?
- How does it impact every major area of your life?
- Your Future Heart Map - Health and wellbeing; Work and Career; Physical Environment; Fun and Recreation; Personal Growth; Relationships and Romance; Financial Security; Family and Friends

Session 10 – HEARTS and SMART Goals

- HEARTS - Harmonious; Enlightened; Authentic; Radiant; Transformative; Service
- SMART – Specific; Measurable; Achievable; Realistic; Timely

Session 11 – Heart Amplification Celebration

- Recap
- Learnings
- Moving forward

"Your timer is limited, so don't waste it living someone else's life. Don't be trapped by dogma – which is living with results of other people's thinking. Don't let the noise of other's opinions drown out your own inner voice and most important have the courage to follow your own heart and intuition"
STEVE JOBS

Smile

Go to the mirror, put your hand on your heart and smile. Look at yourself and say, 'I love you and I am proud of who you are and the journey you are undertaking to live into your best life.'

You were created to live a life truly connected to your heart and embody all the beautiful traits of a human becoming. Remember that everything starts and ends with your heart, step into your new life path with courage, be creative and live with compassion for yourself and all those in your life.

Step 7 – Join Dr John online

It is my great pleasure to personally invite you to join me online at:

- https://www.drjohnmcswiney.com
- Facebook – *The Journey of 100 Hidden Hearts*
- Instagram – @drjohnmcswiney

On these online platforms you will have the opportunity to meet, share stories and journey with like hearted souls.

I will also be guiding you through the Book and showing you how to really connect with your heart at a deeper level, and get the best results to live into your best life.

Join me and let's make this world a better place for you, for me, for our families, friends, and everyone we connect with. Be the change you have been waiting for, and leave a generational legacy of joy, love and compassion.

PART I

THE GENESIS
OF THE HIDDEN
HEART JOURNEY

"Life begins when a person first realises how soon it will end"
MARCELENE COX

"At the end of the day, it's important to know what really matters most in life..., your sanity, your health, your family, and the ability to start anew"
LES BROWN

THE GENESIS OF THE JOURNEY OF 100 HIDDEN HEARTS AND THE MARBLE BOOK OF LIFE

In April 2002, I received an email that touched my heart and had a profound impact on me and it led me to write an unpublished manuscript called *The Marble Book of Life*. It was a short email, and whilst I did not know if it was factual, it resonated deeply in me and I drafted an entire conscious interactive self-empowerment life diary from it.

In essence, the email I received that April contained a story about a man whom I will call Peter. Peter had faced his own mortality and then reflected, not on his past but on transforming his existing life in real time. He decided to live in the moment and created special opportunities for his future.

Peter had been diagnosed with a terminal illness and was told that he did not have long to live *(at best it was no longer than two months)*. He was in his mid 60's, a very successful businessman and by his own admission, a workaholic.

Peter changed his whole life direction, he dropped out of his 'head' and listened to his heart. He created his own 'life count-down clock', which he used to live the life he had always wanted but was too scared to do.

Peter knew that the time he had left was precious and he filled a jar with marbles. Every marble represented a day of his remaining life on Earth and Peter felt into his heart and found compassion for himself. He didn't want to have any regrets, and every day until his death, Peter and his wife Amanda would select a marble from the jar and go on a heart date.

These heart dates were very special, and involved things like spending time with family and friends, sitting on the beach together eating ice-creams, watching the sunsets or anything that gave Peter joy and purpose.

Every time Peter removed a marble from his jar, he would see how much time he had left before he passed. With this simple act, Peter's life suddenly took on new meaning, depth, and significance. He was dying, but his connection with his heart gave him renewed life and a true meaning that was precious to him. The one thing that had been missing in all his working life he found at the very end – his heart!

Peter lived for nearly two months after he was diagnosed and he acknowledged, as did his family and friends, that he was a changed man. He was joyous, loving, caring and empowering of others, often saying that he had been given a second chance; and he genuinely made the most of every moment with an open heart and compassion for himself and those he came into contact with.

♥ **Author's Heartnote:** I have taken the original story and heartened it for this Book. Peter unknowingly dropped out of his head and into his heart, and in a short period of time totally transformed the last days of his existence, living from his heart and into his best life.

Peter was fortunate because, whilst he only truly connected with his heart in his final days, they were days of total compassion, love, joy, forgiveness and spiritual healing for Peter and his family.

What is truly sad is that billions of people move through their lives merely existing and surviving, living small and in fear, with their hearts closed because of traumatic events suffered and endured during their lives. They never experience the compassion and joy that Peter created for himself.

HEARTING QUESTIONS

- *Do you want to be one of these billions of people who just exist and survive?*

- *Do you know you have the choice to connect into your heart, heal, grow and start living into your best life? What exactly are you waiting for?*

- *What will it take for you to find the courage to connect with your heart and truly feel again, and be the human becoming you were always destined to be?*

YOUR LIFE IN A JAR OF MARBLES

Imagine that a jar was placed beside you when you were born, and that it is spiritually connected to you everywhere you go. Your jar has 100 marbles in it, one for every year of your life.

Now imagine that Source (God/Universe) removes a marble from your jar every year, and every year you have a choice to connect with your heart and discover your Hidden Heart and live into your best life.

You have the power within yourself to choose to be the best you can be. This Book has been designed to guide you to reconnect with your heart and live into your best life, a life of compassion and purpose in alignment with your heart.

It is your own life journey that you are creating and living into. The 100 Hidden Hearts are yours. Every marble represents a year of your life, and every year you gift yourself the opportunity to connect with your heart and live a beautiful, compassionate heart-filled life… or not! The choice is yours. It's exciting to know that you have the choice, right now. You have the choice to connect with your heart, and this Book is your personal guide on how to do it.

4

"Trust is like that jar of marbles. What people say and do tells you whether to add or remove a marble. When you assess a relationship, you look to see how full that person's jar is. The people in your life whose jars are overflowing are the ones you keep very close. The ones you offer your deepest trust and love"
BRENE BROWN

HEART ACTIVATION EXERCISE

I invite you to gift yourself a jar and 100 marbles. Make it a Heart Tryst date, and let your heart decide what it truly wants. After you obtain your jar and your marbles, place the jar in a position where you will see it every day.

Put all 100 marbles into the jar. Now remove all the marbles that correspond with your actual age. For example, if you are 54, then remove 54 marbles.

Look at your jar and the marbles that remain. Those marbles represent the years remaining in your life, if you get to 100!

- How does that make you feel?
- Are you truly happy and satisfied with how many life marbles you have already used?
- Do you have any regrets about your life so far?
- Have you lived the life you know you truly want and desire?

MY MARBLE JOURNEY

The story of Peter and his marbles really touched my heart deeply. I knew life was precious as I had lost my younger brother Daniel when he was killed by a drunk driver a week after my 22nd birthday.

I shared Peters story of the marbles with my family and friends as I believed it provided a powerful message; to live your best life through your heart every day and to have a positive compassionate impact on the world around you.

I immediately considered buying a bucket of marbles to start my journey, however at the time I also had my two baby boys in the house and I didn't want either of them discovering the marbles and trying to eat them.

Over the next 12 months I had many ideas about what to do with the marbles; replace them with jelly beans, rocks and even lego bricks! One evening everything clicked and I was inspired to not just have a jar of marbles but to also write a book that would guide people to discover their hearts and live into an empowered heart centered life, one precious marble year at a time.

I set about writing a manuscript called The Marble Book of Life and I drafted an interactive self-empowerment life diary that included paper marbles that could be used to inspire people to be the best they could be.

"Sometimes you will never know the value of a moment until it becomes a memory"
DR SEUSS

"The way I see it, if you want the rainbow you have to put up with the rain"
DOLLY PARTON

5

The idea of *The Marble Book* captured my heart, inspired me and captivated my imagination. I wrote and designed it, had a draft copy printed and even created its own website in 2003. I spoke with family and friends and discussed the possibilities I wanted to create with it.

I had grand plans of creating a movement to help people transform their lives by following their hearts. I was excited and passionate to make this a reality, my heart knew that this was something that I was destined to do.

Fast forward to 2021 - I had spent the next 18 years, 930 weeks and nearly 6600 days of my life going through the motions of raising a family and climbing the corporate ladder; my *Marble Book* had become all but a distant memory.

I had closed off my own heart and the voice in my head told me I wasn't good enough and that nobody would read the book anyway. I chose to let myself become overwhelmed by work, family and financial commitments and I ostensibly lost the essence of what made me special, I lost connection with my heart.

My corporate career was successful, however I paid a heavy price and found myself in companies and working environments that stripped my heart bare. It left me feeling burnt out and emotionally, physically, and spiritually depleted.

To my own detriment I let my head overrule my heart. In doing so I pursued a professional life that I had little genuine love for. I had lost track of what I truly wanted and desired.

The *Marble Book* had literally become an afterthought until one day in early 2019 I found it in a plastic tub in my garage. It looked worse for wear when I spotted it; with pages coming out, the cover torn and the edges scuffed.

I smiled when I saw it as it was like greeting an old friend. I picked it up and flicked through the pages and a flood of memories and feelings cascaded through me to the point that I felt quite emotional.

6

"You must be the change you want to see in the world"
MAHATMA GHANDI

"We do not need magic to change the world, we carry all the power we need inside ourselves already."
J.K. ROWLING

"Change is hard at first, messy in the middle and gorgeous in the end"
ROBIN SHARMA

"A man is not old until his regrets take the place of his dreams"
YIDDISH PROVERB

"Regret is such a short word ... and yet it stretches on forever"
RANATA SUZUKI

"I'd rather regret the things I have done than regret the things I haven't done "
LUCILLE BALL

I loved this Book; I had written it for a purpose and was passionate about it. I was invested and truly connected to it, however like my professional career, I followed my head and not my heart. I had made a choice to put it to the side and I lived a life out of balance with who I really was.

I did not listen to or follow my heart and I did not live the life I truly wanted or desired. To the outside world I was perceived as successful and happy. In reality, the opposite was true. I had become a shell of the man I wanted to be. I did not follow my heart and it nearly killed me.

I spent about 30 minutes reading through the Book and came to the realisation that I had a choice, I could continue my current path that was literally destroying me, or I could choose to follow my heart.

The young man who wrote the *The Marble Book* did it with his heart to help people to connect with theirs. Little did I know that the very person that needed to truly access his heart the most, was me.

I actually gave myself permission to get out of my head and spent time in my heart and listened to what it told me – *start living the life you were always meant to, be compassionate with yourself, be free, be courageous, find your real voice and have NO regrets*!

My heart exploded with energy at the mere feeling of creating these new possibilities for myself and my future. The day after I found my *Marble Book* I made an appointment to see Kate James; a very gifted wellness Life Coach on the Mornington Peninsula close to where I was living. I spent time with Kate and we discussed my life, my values and my dreams.

I had worked in high level executive and C-suite roles in government and the private sector. The one thing I loved in all my roles was mentoring, encouraging, empowering, and coaching people to be the best they could be.

The following week I enrolled in a Diploma and Master Practitioner Life Coaching course studying mBraining,

"Making a big life change is scary. But know what is even scarier? Regret"
UNKNOWN

"I do not regret the things I have done, but those I did not do"
RORY COCHRANE

"There is no sense in punishing your future for the mistakes of your past. Forgive yourself, grow from it and then let it go"
MELANIE KOULOURIS

"The secret of change is to focus all your energy not on fighting the old, but on building the new"
SOCRATES

"Only the wisest and stupidest of men never change"
CONFUCIUS

"How wonderful it is that nobody need wait a single moment before starting to improve the world"
ANNE FRANK

hypnotherapy, time line therapies, parts integration and NLP (Neuro Linguistic Programming) to name but a few and I went from strength to strength.

In my Master Practitioners course I was introduced to the powerful and fascinating world of *m*Braining and *m*BIT (multiple Brain Integration Techniques) by Dr Suzanne Henwood which are at the leading edge of neuroscientific analysis.

In the groundbreaking book by Grant Soosalu and Marvin Oka titled, '*mBraining: Using your Multiple Brains to do cool stuff*', Soosalu and Marvin state that:

> *Over the past decade, the field of neuroscience has discovered we have complex and functional brains in both our heart and gut. Called the cardiac and enteric brains respectively, scientific evidence is emerging that these neural networks exhibit intelligence and wisdom.'*

I invite you now, to take a moment, shut your eyes and say to yourself either out loud or in your mind, "I have a head brain, a heart brain and a gut brain". It sounds incredible, however the evidence from neuroscience on this matter is clear and Soosalu and Marvin state that,

> *"... so many people find it difficult to make any real and lasting change in their lives', because, ... 'for real, deep, generative change to occur it takes all your brains working together, aligned and in the right sequence."*

This was revelatory for me and literally changed my life. I had spent many years at University completing degrees in Social Science (Economics/Politics), Law, Masters of Arts and a PhD-Philosophy. I was admitted to the Supreme Court of Victoria as a Barrister and Solicitor in April 1999.

8

"Never underestimate the power you have to take your life in a new direction"
GERMANY KENT

"I have accepted fear as a part of life – specifically the fear of change... I have gone ahead despite the pounding in the heart that says: turn back"
ERICA JONG

I was a Doctor of Philosophy and a lawyer and considered myself educated, however the discovery that my heart was a brain and that it had its own language, highest expression and that it communicated with me and my other 'brains' literally blew me away.

After studying *m*Braining and *m*BIT, I became a certified *m*BIT practitioner and developed a deeper understanding, respect and appreciation of the critical importance for people, like myself, to go inward, connect with your heart and use this as the basis to start living into your best life.

I imagined being fully connected with my heart and all of my hopes, goals, dreams and desires being in alignment with my 'multiple brains'! I wanted to live into my best life but up until that point I had limited understanding of how that was even possible.

I was disconnected from my heart and it didn't matter how many books I read, how many degrees I possessed, how many letters I had after my name or what C-suite position I held, my life had a hollowness to it. I was wasting my marbles, in fact I wasn't even using them, I was just going through the motions. No heart, no joy and no compassion for myself.

I had made numerous personal and professional life choices and had felt a tug of war. In some cases, a battle between my head, gut and heart and my head and gut always won. I would feel my heart pulling in a particular direction and it felt right however I knowingly went against it. That is the primary reason why I was left unfulfilled professionally and being depleted in other areas of my life.

In 2020 during the Covid pandemic I met a few people who were on a similar journey to myself and I told them about *The Marble Book*. I also sent them the updated draft of my book and they all read the old version as well and commented that the new version had no heart and it felt like the heart was stripped out of it.

It was at this point that I knew that I had been hiding my own heart and it manifested in the revised draft of this Book. The sad

9

"You change your life by changing your heart"
MAX LUCADO

"There comes a time in your life when you have to choose to turn the page, write another book or simply close it"
SHANNON ALDER

"Hope is being able to see that there is light despite all the darkness"
DESMOND TUTU

"When the world says, 'give up', hope whispers, 'try one more time'"
UNKNOWN

"Whenever you find yourself doubting how far you can go. Just remember how far you have come. Remember everything you have faced, all the battles you have won and all the fears you have overcome"
UNKNOWN

truth of the matter was, I had disconnected from my heart, and it was in this moment that my world became a lot clearer.

The missing piece of the original book was the journey to connect with my own Hidden Heart. I discovered as part of my own journey that the book I had written was the guide I needed to help me discover myself.

After a period of deep reflection and contemplation, I felt into my own heart and redrafted the original manuscript and gave it a literal compassionate triple bypass! I incorporated the core theme of *The Marble Book* and fused it with the powerful messages, tools and hearting exercises that are now a key part of this Book and my own heart connection programs that I run with people all over the world.

The Book now has an energy and a designed purpose to empower people to reconnect with their heart space and use their multiple brains, especially their hearts, to affect meaningful change in their lives.

The Book contains information that you may have studied and read about, or even heard about on your life's journey. All information and learnings that you come across do have a meaning, even if you don't understand the significance at the time. The overwhelming majority of our 'learnings' are head based and head dominated. This Book is heart based and heart dominated, and you are invited to approach and experience this Book in a very different way and with a very different feel and energy than you would reading and learning from another text. It is a beautiful journey and one that will enrich your life because it is grounded, gentle and compassionate.

I am excited for what the future holds because the world definitely needs more heart; an abundance of heart in people's decision making will see an exponential increase in peace, forgiveness, hope, joy, trust, connection, appreciation, gratitude, equanimity, emotional security, love, generosity, emotional truth,

10

"It is on the strength of observation and reflection that one finds a way. So, we must dig and delve unceasingly"
CLAUDE MONET

"You attract what you are, not what you want. So, if you want it then reflect it"
TONY GASKINS

compassion and wisdom. Imagine a world where this was the prevailing orthodoxy?

The exciting thing is that you have the power within you right now to hearten your life and hearten your world. My dream is for every person in the world to align themselves and deeply reconnect with their hearts. My mission is to connect every person with their hearts and as I have stated earlier, this is a legacy mission.

I invite you to realign yourself and reconnect with the amazing person you already are. I invite you to come from your heart and be the best version of you in all ways. A human becoming with true authentic connection and compassion for yourself and the world around you.

So now is your chance to start living an aligned heart filled life and create opportunities for what you want to do with your next marble, and the next, and the next, and the next … be compassionate, be creative, be courageous and take action to transform your life today.

Life is an incredible gift so make the most of it and always remember that everything starts and ends with your heart!

"Focus. Don't settle. Don't waste time. Don't be distracted you have goals to accomplish. Go and make it happen"
UNKNOWN

"Don't reinvent the wheel, just realign it"
ANTHONY D'ANGELO

"Sometimes you need to step outside, get some air, and remind yourself of who you are and where you want to be"
UNKNOWN

11

PART II

YOUR HIDDEN

HEART JOURNEY

BEGINS

14   *"The Clock of Life – The Clock of life is wound but once, and no man has the power to tell just when the hands will stop at late or early. Today, only if our own. So live, love and toil with a will. Place no faith in tomorrow, for the clock may soon be still"*
ROBERT H. SMITH

Are you ready to take your first steps to find your Hidden Heart and live into your best life?

TIME TO LOOK AT YOUR LIFE HEART CLOCK

I invite you to go to Part VI of the Book and have a look at the page that corresponds with your current age and consider the following:

- look at your marble jar and see how many marbles you have left in your marble jar of life
- look at your Heart Clock and the time you have already lived in your life
- look at the time you have left in your life "if" you live to 100!

How do you feel when you see your life represented like this?
What feelings and emotions are coming up for you?
Do you truly feel you have lived into your best life?

BALANCED HEART BREATHING

Balanced Heart breathing is a powerful breathing exercise designed to align you with your heart and to open your higher consciousness to receive understanding, knowledge, and wisdom.

I invite you to always start with balanced heart breathing before you do any exercise or activity outlined in this Book as it will ensure that you are in flow and balanced in order to receive the maximum benefit of what you are engaged with. Ok, let's do some breathing:

1. Sit or lie flat in a comfortable position (or if you cannot, gently ground yourself in place) and close your eyes.

2. Put one hand on your belly just below your ribs and the other hand on your chest just over your heart space.

3. Take a deep breath in through your nose for 6 seconds and let your belly push your hand out. Your chest should not move. (Imagine your belly is a balloon and you are blowing it up.)

4. Breathe out through closed lips for 6 seconds as if you were whistling. Feel the hand on your belly move in.

5. (*Optional but highly recommended*) – as you breathe in imagine that each breath has a color associated with it and that this color also contains energy and power that is calming and healing for you. Every breath you inhale contains this powerful colorful healing energy. Breathe it into your heart space and into your belly and feel it flow through your entire body. Feel the power and the energy release inside you with every breath. Now imagine that when you are breathing out that every breath out contains within it, the stress, the tension, the anxiety, the pain, the fear, the hurt, the torment and any other negative feeling, emotion or limiting belief that you are holding inside of you. Breathe these negative energies out and release them to the Universe.

6. Do this breathing until you feel a sense of calm and peace, then feel into your heart space and ask your heart for guidance. Ask what it truly wants and desires.

7. Notice how you feel at the end of the exercise.

Also, when you are feeling stressed, fearful or anxious about an issue or problem and you need guidance or clarification on something, I invite you to take a moment and do your balanced heart breathing and really feel into what your heart truly wants and desires.

HEART CONNECTION OATH

It is very important that you feel into your heart and genuinely acknowledge the level of time and commitment that you are going to gift yourself on this adventure.

Your Hidden Heart journey is not a part time pursuit or something that you do when you are bored. It is a metaphysical lifestyle choice where you are gifting yourself permission to embark on a journey to reconnect and activate your Heart. This is an expedition to uncover your own Hidden Heart.

On your journey to find your Hidden Heart I invite you to sign your name, and your heart, to your very own Heart Connection Oath.

Your Heart Connection Oath refers to the degree to which you are committed to actually achieve what your heart truly desires for you. It is an instrument to help you move towards living into your best life.

I have chosen an Oath instead of a contract because an Oath is a powerful heartfelt manifestation of intent. An Oath is a solemn promise about your behavior and your actions, and it comes from a deep place of knowing, love, and commitment. A contract is a head-based document and whilst it may carry legal weight, it is of little use to you when connecting with your heart.

I invite you to complete your Heart Connection Oath and when you have signed it I would like you to stand in front of a mirror and read it out loud to yourself. When you do this, really feel into what feelings and emotions (if any) come up and make a note of them in our journal.

16

"Your heart is the softest place on earth. Take care of it"
NAYYIRAH WAHEED

"The most beautiful things in the world cannot be seen or even touched, they must be felt with the heart"
HELEN KELLER

"The emotion that can break your heart is sometimes the very one that heals it"
NICHOLAS SPARKS

"When confronted with a challenge, the committed heart will search for a solution. The undecided heart searches for an escape"
ANDY ANDREWS

"Commitment is what transforms a promise into reality"
ABRAHAM LINCOLN

Now that you have your signed your Heart Connection Oath, I invite you to find a heartbeat buddy and tell them what you are doing. Read your Heart Connection Oath to them and ask them to help make you accountable.

HEART CONNECTION OATH

I, ..., place my hand on my heart and swear that:

- I will fully invest myself into undertaking an intensive, compassionate, and guided encounter with my heart
- I will commit to read *The Journey of 100 Hidden Hearts*
- I will commit to feel into my heart and undertake all Hidden Heart Whispers, Hidden Heart Trysts, and the completion of all the Hidden Hearting exercises and activation tasks contained in the Book
- I will be emotionally and spiritually available for everything I need to do
- I will be courageous, creative, compassionate, and authentic
- I will be truthful and respectful with myself and others
- I will be honest with myself and others
- I will be fully present during my heart connection journey
- I will establish an exceptional self-care practice
- I will be available for my Heartbeat Buddy

....
Signature

....
Date

♥ **Author's Heartnote:** I invite you to consider the fact that signing your Heart Connection Oath and actually fulfilling it are two different things. You will always have the choice in what you decide to do and not do. However, please know this, if you never choose to go inwards and connect with your heart, you will miss out on discovering how to live into your best life and that would be a tragedy. The only thing of significance and importance here is how you truly want to live your life! How important is it to you?

17

Congratulations on completing your Heart Connection Oath and making the choice to value yourself and take the first steps to connect with your heart space.

At the start of your journey I would like to invite you to feel into the following hearting questions and write your responses in your journal or in the Book, whatever feels best for you.

HEARTING QUESTIONS

- *Why do you want to connect with your heart?*

- *What are your expectations of connecting with your heart?*

- *What do you want to achieve by connecting with your heart?*

- *What are your fears in connecting with your heart?*

- *How much time do you spend in your heart during a normal day? (Your heart is compassion)*

- *What has been the major theme in your life over the past year? Has your heart been present in this?*

HEART ACTIVATION EXERCISES

In the Book you will encounter heart activation exercises and questions that have been specifically designed to reconnect you with your heart. All of these activation exercises and questions are optional and it will be your choice whether to complete them, or not.

Your life is a series of choices and the sooner you find the courage to connect with your heart, the sooner your life begins to reflect the core essence of who you truly are.

I would like to take this opportunity to invite you to please remember that you are worthy to step into your destiny as your best self, living from your heart with compassion for yourself and those in your life.

Your personal journey will be inherently strengthened by the following two heart activation exercises which I have named your Heart Trysts and Heart Whispers. Many years ago I read Julia Cameron's magnificent book, 'The Artists Way'. If you have not already read it, please do yourself a favour and do so.

In her book Julia invites you to go on an artist's date and to write morning pages. Both exercises are powerful tools for artists (and others) to use to help them stimulate their creative juices. When you stimulate your creativity, it emanates from your head brain. The highest expression of your head brain is 'creativity' and that's why it is so successful.

Your heart is a brain and it has its own language and communicates with your other multiple brains including you. Your hearts highest expression and vibration is compassion. Your Heart Trysts and Heart Whispers have been designed to connect you directly with your compassionate and insightful heart.

Heart Trysts and Heart Whispers are powerful practices that have been designed to gently reengage and connect you with your heart. Over time you will strengthen that bond, and this will enable you to live a life with greater compassion, love, empathy, kindness, and humanity.

"Life is a matter of choices, and every choice you make, makes you"
JOHN C. MAXWELL

"Life presents many choices, the choices we make determine our future"
CATHERINE PULSIFER

19

HIDDEN HEART TRYSTS

A Heart Tryst is a date that you have with your heart. Your tryst should last for around an hour and it is an essential part of aligning you to your hearts true purpose.

Your Heart Tryst is to be undertaken at least once a week. It is an exercise in self-love that is designed to connect you with your heart and your inner self at a deeper level. You are literally asking your heart what it truly wants and desires. Your heart is empowered when compassion is present:

- Commence with your balanced heart breathing until you are feeling relaxed and calm
- Feel into your heart space and ask your heart the following question, '*My beautiful heart, what do you truly want and desire for me to do to connect into you today?*' '*Heart, give me insight as to how I can serve you and honour what the Universe requires from me.*'
- Once your heart has communicated what it truly wants to do, make the time and do it

Your tryst should last for around an hour and I invite you to write a list of your future Heart Trysts (big and small) and plan to have fun.

HIDDEN HEART WHISPERS

Your Heart Whispers are an exercise in automatic writing that provide your heart with an opportunity to connect to Source and express itself via the written word.

Your heart brain communicates with your other multiple brains every second of every day. It has its own language, and it controls every aspect of your existence. Heart Whispers are a beautiful and unique way of feeling into your heart and giving expression to your heart's true wants and desires.

20 ♥ **Author's Heartnote:** your first Heart Tryst is for you to make a time and feel into buying yourself a special journal and pen with which to undertake your Hidden Heart journey. It is essential that you feel into your heart and follow its lead.

I highlighted Julia Cameron's beautiful work 'The Artists Way' earlier. Julia's morning pages are a powerful way for people to connect with their creative self and this is primarily through your head and your mind. The highest expression of your head brain is creativity, and this style of writing and expression is perfect for that level of connection.

Heart Whispers have been designed to go much deeper; into your very being, into your grace. They are a very powerful technique that when practiced daily will unlock and empower your journey of full heart discovery. Your heart is empowered when its voice is heard and felt:

- You need a beautiful journal and a beautiful pen (*You should already have these from your first Hidden Heart Tryst*)
- Clear at least 15-30 minutes a day at a time that is best for you to experience this transformative exercise.
- Commence with your balanced heart breathing until you are feeling relaxed and calm
- Feel into your heart space
- Start writing anything and everything that is being presented from your heart until there is nothing more to say. (I refer to this as your daily Heart Whisper)
- It is important not to read what you have written until the end of every month.
- Prior to starting a new month on your Hidden Heart journey, I invite you to read over your Heart Whispers and look for key messages, words, phrases, themes and issues that were present in your whispers.
- Your Heart Whispers will help guide you in what is happening in and around your life from your hearts perspective and give you insight into the areas you need to explore to possibly address, heal and grow.

PART III

THE METAPHYSICAL FRAMEWORK TO CONNECT YOU WITH YOUR HIDDEN HEART

In 2020 the planet went into a global Covid lockdown and billions of people around the world were forced to come to terms not only with a global pandemic but their own mortality as well.

The Covid lockdowns provided an opportunity for people to reflect on what was important in their lives. Millions of souls took a step back and genuinely realised that they wanted more than just surviving, they truly desired to live a life with greater compassion, meaning and purpose.

On your life journey, especially one to discover your Hidden Heart there is a metaphysical framework; a map, that I would invite you to consider engaging with because it will transform you and how you live your life.

The framework is based on your Hidden Heart Diamond and it is a powerful tool that will enable you to connect with your heart, gain a deeper appreciation of self and provide you with the opportunity to discover your own Hidden Heart and live into your best life.

Are you living your best life right now?

Are you truly connected to your heart?

Are you genuinely happy with your world?

How many more years are you going to spend just existing in the life you are in now?

You have a choice, do nothing, or take heartfelt action and reclaim you and your life by following your own heart. When you connect with your heart you will open it to deeply feel everything transform and change in your world. You will free your heart to:

- Awaken and connect with your true self
- Navigate inner woundings and traumas
- Acknowledge and honour your heart space
- Notice and observe emotional patterns
- Truly love yourself
- Awaken your hidden heart
- Manage your Ego
- Reconnect and reparent your inner child
- Increase your self-worth and self-belief
- Release what has weighed you down (emotionally and spiritually)
- Realign your mind, body, and soul
- Experience a true sense of positive empowerment
- Feel genuine compassion and empathy
- Improve all relationships (personal, intimate, and professional)
- Forgive yourself and others
- Heal past wounds and traumas
- Acknowledge, embrace, and feel into your intuition

WHAT IS YOUR HIDDEN HEART DIAMOND?

Your Hidden Heart Diamond is a basic and simple form; however it manifests as a powerful symbol of significance. Spiritually, the diamond signifies immortality and trusting in yourself, the symbolism of the diamond carries energy and messaging relating to rebirth, revival, and transformation.

Diamonds are seen as light, life and the sun. It represents faithfulness, love, purity, innocence, and relationships filled with love. Diamonds promote and inspire creativity, ingenuity, inventiveness, originality, faith, and endurance as well as helping to manifest abundance in all areas of your life.

"[The universe] cannot be read until we have learnt the language and become familiar with the characters in which it is written. It is written in mathematical language, and the letters are triangles, circles and other geometrical figures, without which means it is humanly impossible to comprehend a single word; without which one wanders in vain through a dark labyrinth."
QUOTE ATTRIBUTED TO GALILEO GALILEI 1564-1642

25

The diamond shape (or rhombus) is symbolic of illumination and being fully awakened in all parts of your existence – Mind; Body; Heart; Soul; Ego.

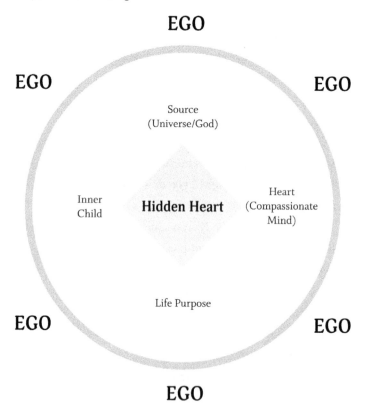

Hidden Heart Diamond

You become awakened in these areas of your life to fully shine in the world. You were created to stand in the light and your journey is about preparing you to know that you truly belong there. You are breaking free of your very limited conscious potential and moving into becoming the You you were always destined to be.

The top part of the Diamond reflects your spiritual body, it is Source (Universe/God) and the lower part of the Diamond represents your physical body and relates to the earth and your life path. It is the yin and the yang. This geometric symbol, your diamond represents the inner focus that you need to discover and evolve during this lifetime.

Your journey is to walk your path, live into your purpose and connect with your heart to reinstall balance within yourself. The diamond shape represents the ideal of a human being that has achieved this inner balance. The yin and yang in harmony brought about by compassion, honesty, healing, and growth.

HIDDEN HEART DIAMOND QUESTIONS AND ACTIVATION STATEMENTS

On your journey to finding your Hidden Heart I invite you to memorise your Hidden Heart Diamond and gently feel into the following Hidden Heart Diamond questions and activation statements:

- *Am I connected to Source?*

- *Am I connected to my Heart?*

- *Am I connected to my Inner Child?*

- *Where is my Ego?*

- *Am I living into my Life Purpose?*

- *What is my Hidden Heart?*

These Hidden Heart Diamond questions and activation statements are powerful tools that you will use to help guide you on your path to connect with all of you and lead you to your Hidden Heart.

Now let's look at all the elements that make up your Hidden Heart Diamond:

- Source (God/Universe)
- Heart (Compassionate Mind)
- Inner Child
- Life Purpose
- Hidden Heart - is found in the center of the diamond (It is your X Factor, your soul purpose)
- Ego

YOUR HIDDEN HEART (METAPHYSICAL PERSPECTIVE)

"The human heart has hidden treasures, in secret kept, in silence sealed: The thoughts, the hopes, the dreams, the pleasures, whose charms were broken if revealed"
CHARLOTTE BRONTE

"Every heart has a beautiful hidden story that desires to be expressed"
DR JOHN MCSWINEY

"Your heart has its reasons which reason knows not"
BLAISE PASCA

In your Hidden Heart Diamond, you will see that at the very center of the diamond is your hidden heart which represents the core of who you are, it is associated with the essence of your very being.

Your heart is your doorway to your soul and when you connect with it you reunite with the wisdom and intelligence that resides deep within you. They are connected and whilst your soul is always shining within you, your hidden heart (like your heart) can become obscured, lost, and disconnected from you.

Your hidden heart space is unique to you, it is sacred, and it develops, evolves, and grows even if you are unaware of it. It exists in union with your soul as it is the human or physical essence of your soul and can be symbolically linked to the world around you.

Your human body is a part of the natural world and just like the natural world you come into existence in a physical form. You learn, grow, and mature over time. Your life journey is punctuated by you spending time in your own emotional, physical, and spiritual wilderness and it is imperative that you do this so that you can feel into your heart and soul on a deeper level.

If your soul is your direct conduit to Source, then your hidden heart is that metaphysical bridge that connects your soul to You and is how you then live your life through your physical body at your highest compassionate expression.

Your hidden heart is not a shadow, it is not dark, negative, malevolent, destructive, or harmful to you or those who you relate to in your life.

As a spiritual being you have been created to transform and evolve. To do this when you connect with your hidden heart you uncover those powerful parts of your soul that lift your vibration and frequency to higher levels of consciousness and being.

The awakening of your consciousness into your hidden heart occurs when you connect with all of you and feel into that deep inner knowing that compels you to reveal and discover the truth that lies behind the outer veil of appearances you have created to protect you from yourself.

Your roadmap to your hidden heart is found in your Hidden Heart Diamond and it has been designed to take you from feeling like who you think you *should be,* to who you know you are *meant to* be. Your hidden heart evolves with you and can be observed and felt deeply within you when you are in flow at all your Hidden Heart Diamond points in your life.

Your hidden heart is strongly aligned with your soul and whilst it is directly connected with Source energy, your hidden heart is grounded in you as a human becoming. In this Book, the underlying symbolism is that every one of your hypothetical 100 years of life is accompanied by a hidden heart that is waiting to be discovered to bring you closer to not just who you should be but also to who you are meant to be.

When you feel into your heart and follow your light it will guide you home and when you feel into and connect with your Diamond it will lead you to your Hidden Heart.

I invite you to engage with every aspect of your Hidden Heart Diamond and truly gift yourself the time and the opportunity to connect with your heart and live into your best life.

I wish you nothing but success on your journey of self-discovery.

"Deep in the heart every mystery is hidden"
RUMI

"When you are evolving to a higher self, the road seems lonely but you're simply shedding the energies that no longer match the frequency of your destiny"
UNKNOWN

"When you contact the higher self, the source of power within, you tap into a reservoir of infinite power"
DEEPAK CHOPRA

"Never fear your higher self"
TONE LEE

SOURCE (GOD/UNIVERSE)

Source, spirit, energy, life-force, God, the Universe and Higher Self are but a few of the main descriptors and expressions that you use to connect with Source. There is no right path to encounter freedom of Source for every soul is different just as every fingerprint is different.

You are a grand design preprogrammed with the ability to make decisions and to exercise freedom of choice together with the innate ability to heal yourself.

You are a fusion of elements such as mind, body, spirit, and they all co-exist with the highest expression to align in wisdom for you to find your true purpose and Hidden Heart.

You will be exploring these divine elements and in doing so you will be able to fully utilise them to realise your true spiritual power at the highest level for yourself and the world around you.

You have been sent many spiritual messengers to teach and help you comprehend and understand your purpose in relation to aligning your higher self with Source. It is through this alignment that spiritual maturity is achieved. These spiritual guides have provided you with many spiritual tools to align you with Source in your everyday life.

The greatest gift that Source has bestowed upon you is that of choice and free will. This one simple yet incredibly powerful gift provides you with the power to control your world. Through the gift of choice and free will you empower yourself to step forward into your destiny.

In relation to the Hidden Heart Diamond, the vehicle to establishing a connection with Source is through your own spiritual practice which is different for everyone.

Your connection to Source will be enhanced exponentially when you develop your spiritual gifts, and this will enable you on a personal level to have greater insights into your hidden heart.

30

♥ **Author's Heartnote:** In relation to spirituality, my intention is not to label or proselytize religion or faith for that is an individual choice. If you are not a spiritual person then I invite you to consider Source, in the context of this Book, as more akin to transcendence and a transcendent state.

I invite you to continue your development in this area for the rest of your life as there is always room to learn, and I encourage you to see this as an amazing opportunity for your spiritual self-development.

Let's revisit the concept that … **You are a spiritual being having the human experience** as it leads us into creating precious time for you to start truly recognising and embracing your innate spiritual gifts.

You are on this journey of discovery, and this is your chance to step up and claim what has always been yours. It is time for you to truly acknowledge that your spiritual gifts will enable you to see and feel things from a completely different perspective and energy level.

When you live in your flow, follow your heart, connect with your inner child, manage your ego, and connect with Source. Your spiritual gifts will come to the fore so be ready to embrace who you truly are.

To deny your innate spiritual gifts is like trying to swim upstream against the current. You will be alright for a little while, but you will begin to tire, and it will become harder and harder to move at all.

In this section on Source, you will be exploring a few key practical and spiritual ways to help you change and transform your world. It will be a safe and secure place to explore, so open your heart and make the choice to connect with Source.

SPIRITUAL DARKNESS AND SHADOW

Where there is light there is darkness and shadow. It is important on your journey to acknowledge and recognise this. It is also normal to feel the darkness (shadow work).

It is beneficial to know the impact and role that this plays in your spiritual journey. I remember when I first met Matthew. He had been on his own spiritual journey for a few years and had

"No matter how long the room has been dark, an hour or a million years, the moment the lamp of awareness is lit the entire room becomes luminous"
TENZIN WANGYAL RINPOCHE

"Knowing your own darkness is the best method for dealing with other people"
CARL JUNG

"You are a being of light and just like a star, it is in the darkness that you will shine the brightest"
UNKNOWN

been through a very painful experience in business (ironically in the wellness industry).

Matthew had lost everything, including his marriage. His story was tragic, however it resonated with me in relation to this area because his ex-business partner was an old school friend and had gambled away the company, then covered it up.

Matthew spent two years working closely with his ex-business partner and knew intuitively that something was wrong as there was a major disconnect between his business partners words and actions. His business partner was a respected person in the wellness and wholistic community who often spoke about living from the light, however he was living from Ego and shadow. Light will always prevail, but it exists with darkness and shadow.

It is a truism that love is light, but it does not exist in a vacuum. I believe you can live into your best life through your heart and an important part of that is truly recognising that darkness and shadow exists as well. By acknowledging and accepting this truism, it will set you free to trust your intuition and enable you to explore your own unique space that you want to live into. It will also empower you not to be deceived by those who masquerade in the light but are themselves wholly Ego and shadow.

In life you experience moments that test you to your very core when you feel surrounded and/or consumed by darkness. It is in these moments that you need to feel into and recognise the light that exists within you. This light is connected to Source, and it is through your connection to Source that will lift you out of the darkness.

When you connect to Source it will help change your perceptions of self, your relationships, your friendships, your career, and your relationship with Source itself which is essential for your own development, healing, and growth.

Once you are connected to your light you begin to grow with it, and into it, getting stronger every day on a spiritual level. It is time for you to lead with the light.

32

"It takes great faith in the unknown to investigate the dark places in our own being"
ADYASHANTI

"You are the light within your own darkness"
STACIE

HOW TO CONNECT TO SOURCE

Your connection with Source is a deeply personal experience and one that should be cherished. There are many ways in which you can connect with Source and hear and feel and experience the way that Source interacts and communicates with You.

When you step into your own light and truth you activate this and the easiest way to connect with Source is to acknowledge that Source exists and just speak and feel from your heart. Have a conversation (prayer, meditate, sing) and speak your truth; pour out your heart and ask for help, support, comfort, guidance, and direction. Prayer is powerful and should be embraced as part of your life.

SPIRITUAL SYNCHRONICITIES AND SIGNS

Synchronistic activities are the connections between yourself and Source that are being realised and presented in physical form to you. When you recognise your synchronicities, they can be powerful signs and guidance and assist you on your life journey.

Source communicates with you in synchronistic ways, and this happens over and over in repetitive ways, and this happens so Source can reinforce a message as being beyond just mere coincidence.

Spiritual signs surround you and you encounter them on a regular basis. When you choose to open your heart and your connection with Source these signs start to manifest like signposts in your life.

I invite you to imagine a 3D artwork that is made up of thousands of little dots and you stare and stare at it and it doesn't look like anything. You walk past the artwork for days and even weeks and still see nothing but little dots, and then all of a sudden something happens and what appeared as just thousands of random dots become a beautiful image.

❤ **Authors Heartnote:** When I talk about prayer, I would invite you to feel into it from a non-denominational perspective. You do not have to be a member of a religion, church, group, culture etc to pray. The word has been misappropriated and marginalized to the extent that it has been devalued because of its association with organised religion. It is powerful and should be used and respected whenever you feel you need to connect with Source.

"There is a higher more powerful part of you. Your higher self will come through your intuition, coincidences, and synchronicities of all kinds"
JAMES VAN PRAAGH

"The Universe is not outside of you. Look inside yourself. Everything that you want, you already are"
RUMI

This is what happens when you connect to Source and allow yourself to see and feel the signs and synchronicities that you encounter every day. When you connect and start to see these signs it is very important that you really focus on their specific meanings as they relate to You. What were you thinking and feeling at the time you encountered these signs and synchronicities?

Here are the most common passive signs and symbols of Source communication for you to be aware of:

- **Geometric shapes** – triangles are associated with concepts such as power, stability, and the Holy Trinity; circles represent wholeness and a natural sense of completion and can even signify eternity and constant movement.
- **White feathers** – white feathers often appear in your life when you are undergoing a spiritual transformation and change. They are associated to the Angelic realm and can show that you are on your right path.
- **Coins** – finding coins is considered a sign of good fortune and foretells that something good is about to happen to you. Coins also show up as reminders you are on the right path and are being guided by Source. Coins will also have a number on them and can be related back to specific Angel numbers for deeper meanings.
- **Animals and insects** – spirit animals and insects are all around you and when animals and insects cross your path it can be a sign from Source; they are often sent to guide, teach, and communicate with you. Any time you come across an animal or an insect and feel that it is not random or a coincidence, take the time to feel into the experience and if there is a deeper meaning.
- **Numbers** – you are surrounded by numbers and Source uses them to communicate with you. Numbers have special spiritual significance and if you are seeing a repeating number sequence such as 1111 or 7777 etc. Source is trying

to get your attention about something so jump online and Google their Angelic meaning.

The signs and symbols above have been termed by me as passive because of the nature in which you encounter them. There are other signs and symbols which I term as 'active' because you set your intention with Source and see what transpires. I invite you to test the following:

- Feel into your heart
- Set your question/intention and make it unambiguous
- Request a specific sign or symbol to confirm, verify or acknowledge your request.

"Spiritual signs are all around you. Open your heart and your soul to believe as well as receive"
CATH AKESSON

35

HEARTING EXERCISES AND QUESTIONS

Observe any signs and synchronicities in your journal.

Ask for a sign for something to happen in your life and then wait for it to happen.

Observe the moments of darkness and practice the meditation (below).

How often do you communicate with Source?

Continue with your Heart Whispers and Heart Trysts. Observe the ebb and flow of your life. Do not be afraid of it; embrace it.

SOURCE CONNECTION MEDITATION

Prepare your Body Spiritually to heal:

1. I invite you to see a powerful and healing Golden light appear above your head. Allow the light to enter your crown chakra, travel down your spine, through your

body, down to your feet and into the ground. This golden light is being poured into you from every expanding Lotus leaf that you have created with the sole purpose of healing your spiritual body.

2. I invite you to see a powerful and healing silver stream of light emerging from the ground under your feet and travelling up your legs, through your spine and going into the lotus leaf at the point above your head.

3. You have now established a powerful healing energetic circuit. I want you to see and feel both energies travelling up and down your spine. Allow this energy to slowly expand through your body out past your physical being, burning up all negative, adverse, damaging, harmful and self-destructive thoughts, feelings and emotions that limit you in any way.

4. I now invite you to see and feel the energy flowing through you become one huge circular healing force around your body sealing your whole energy field. This energy field is a place of safety, security, growth, and healing.

5. When you are ready, I invite you to place your hands on your body in any place where you feel needs to be healed. Imagine that the silver and gold energy flowing through your body, meeting at your heart and then exploding into a huge vibrating stream of healing light that you will now use to heal yourself.

6. Use this stream of healing light for yourself and others in your life and imagine your healing stream entering their bodies healing them as it heals you.

7. When you feel you have completed your healing slowly bring your hands together and place them over your heart. Breathe deeply, bringing your stream back into an easily managed flow and when you are ready open your eyes and feel into your healing experience.

8. Also, be aware that the healing energy field you have created is still activated around you and if you desire, you can spend your time in this state and continue your healing. The choice is yours.

YOUR SENSES AND YOUR SIXTH SENSE

Your intuition will help guide you to a greater and deeper understanding of who you are and help you unlock yourself and the world around you.

The human body has five primary senses: sight, hearing, touch, taste, and smell. However, recent scientific discoveries in the neurological field have identified nine or more senses, and some list as many as twenty-one.

The neuroscientific discoveries are quite incredible, and you can read about them if you desire, however we are primarily focused in the Book on your sixth sense.

The idea of a sixth sense is that in addition to these five core senses that everybody is aware of, you also possess a sixth sense that is attuned to very subtle, non-physical sensations, frequencies, vibrations and energy.

Your sixth sense is sometimes described as intuition, or the sense of knowing something without previous stored knowledge about it. To put it simply, your sixth sense refers to your ability to perceive something that is not apparently there, such as when you get a sense that something is about to happen even though you cannot fully explain what may transpire.

You literally sense that something is about to occur that will impact upon you and your life. It is important to also acknowledge that when aligned with your heart chakra, the two areas work hand in hand to offer you a guidance system that will never let you down.

It is also fascinating to note that in Heartmath studies it has been shown that all information we receive is first processed by

"We each have a sixth sense that is attuned to the oneness dimension in life, providing a means for us to guide our lives in accord with our ideas"
HENRY REED

"Faith is a kind of sixth sense which works in cases which are without the purview of reason"
MAHATMA GANDHI

the heart and it is your heart that sets up your system for fight, flight, or the relaxation of your Autonomic Nervous System (ANS). The flow of information through your body starts with your heart then flows to your head, and then to your gut to produce a body response.

Unfortunately, society in general has remained out of touch and has chosen to remain oblivious to the importance of your intuition. Many in society would have you believe that following your heart will not fully serve you as it is somehow irrational, over emotional, and unpredictable.

Remember that everything starts and ends with your heart, and when followed, it will never let you down especially when you make your connection with Source.

I would also highlight the Chakras that are directly linked to Source; your Crown and Third Eye Chakras.

CROWN CHAKRA

The chakras are what Hindu spiritual traditions describe as the seven centers of concentrated metaphysical energies that are positioned and aligned from the base of your spine to the crown at the top of your head.

The word 'chakra' is Sanskrit for 'wheel' and each chakra is believed to vibrate at its own frequency in a circular pattern that directs energy from the universe into your body's energetic system and as such represents a powerful force to be understood and integrated, by you, into your life.

Your Crown chakra is your seventh chakra and is located at the top of your head; it sits like a crown above your head, hence its name. The dominant color of your crown chakra is white, although it can also be seen as deep purple; it is associated with the following psychological and behavioral characteristics:

38   ♥ **Author's Heartnote:** I would also highlight that the most obvious chakra is your Heart Chakra and that is covered in detail in the Heart (Compassionate Mind) section of the Hidden Heart Diamond.

• Consciousness
• Wisdom
• Connection with the limitless
• Realisation and liberation from limiting patterns
• Relationship with higher states of consciousness
• Ecstasy, bliss
• Presence

When your Crown chakra is out of balance, it can reveal itself as:
• Disconnection to Source
• Constant cynicism regarding what is sacred
• Disconnection from your body and earthly matters
• Closed-mindedness and/or living from your head

Your Crown chakra has been described as the gateway to your cosmic self or your divine self and to your universal consciousness. It is strongly linked to the infinite and the Universal and is essential in helping you connect with Source.

Your Crown chakra will let you access great clarity and enlightened wisdom. When you immerse yourself in the energy of your crown chakra, you will feel a state of peaceful union with all that is, a spiritual ecstasy, but only if you choose to do so.

THIRD EYE CHAKRA

Your third eye chakra is your sixth chakra and is located on your forehead, right between your eyebrows, not in the middle of your forehead. It is your center of intuition and foresight.

The key function of your third eye chakra is focused on the principles of openness and imagination and its dominant color is purple or bluish purple. The images associated with your third eye chakra are an upside-down triangle and the lotus flower and it is associated with the following psychological and behavioural characteristics:

1. Vision
2. Intuition
3. Perception of subtle dimensions and movements of energy
4. Psychic abilities related to clairvoyance and clairaudience especially
5. Access to mystical states such as illumination
6. Connection to wisdom and insight
7. Motivation, inspiration and creativity

When your third eye chakra is out of balance, it can reveal itself as:

- Being stuck in your daily grind
- An inability for you to set goals or a guiding vision for yourself or your life
- Rejection of everything spiritual or beyond the usual
- Not being aware of the bigger picture
- Lack of clarity

Your third eye chakra is your own personal spiritual lens that helps you perceive the more subtle aspects of your reality. I invite you to note that this goes beyond the other five senses and really intersects and moves into the realm of the more refined energies.

Your intuitive awareness and inner perception will be expanded when you awaken and engage with your third eye. It connects your heart with Source and provides you with a special way of seeing and perceiving the images that are presented only to your third eye chakra.

When you focus your heart and consciousness you will see beyond the distractions and illusions that are right in front of you; you will have more insight, understanding and knowledge to live and create a life more deeply aligned with your highest good.

You have an amazing tool at your disposal to help guide you into living your best life with a potent inner knowing. You are already pre-equipped with an inbuilt intuitive antenna that is powerful, reliable, and fully attuned to keep you on your true path. I invite you to start living into discovering and becoming more attune to your intuition.

Is this something that you are prepared to do in your life?

DEVELOPING YOUR INTUITION

Every person has natural intuitive abilities that will help connect You with Source. You will not know where your strengths are until you fully explore them with a sense of fun, an open heart, and a playful attitude.

Your gifts are like a muscle and like any muscle you need to exercise it daily for it to grow and strengthen. This is a beautiful part of your journey and I invite you to fully embrace it and make a connection with Source that will manifestly change your life.

Would you like to know what some of the more well-known intuitive gifts are? You may have even been experiencing them without you being consciously aware:

- Dreams and dream interpretation
- Intuitive healings – reading auras
- Basic mediumship
- Psychometry – reading objects
- Tarot cards
- Remote healings and readings
- Divination tools (pendulums)
- Scrying (look into a crystal ball or fire, tea leaves, subtleties in body Ku - (Pendulum)
- Basic understanding of the four Clairs (Clair meaning 'Voice')

"Intuition is your soul whispering the truth to your heart and hoping that you hear"
KATE SPENCER

"The more you trust your intuition the more empowered you become. The stronger you become and the happier you become"
GISELE BUNDCHEN

THE FOUR CLAIRS

Source communicates with you through your Clair's (meaning 'voice'), and it relies upon you to use your intuition as a special conduit to receive spiritual messages and guidance. The four Clairs are:

1. **Clairaudience (hearing voices)**

   Clairaudience is the intuitive ability to hear beyond the normal hearing range. If you are clairaudient you receive messages and intuitive information directly from Source via hearing.

   The messages and information you receive can be presented to you in many forms. You may hear faint unintelligible sounds, names, phrases, particular words, or even music.

   When you start to allow yourself to feel into this gift you may notice a distinct ringing or changes of pressure in your ears, such as popping or buzzing noises or you may start to hear voices.

   These voices can sound different from the voices you normally hear and it can sound like the voice is coming from a person who is right beside you, inside your head or even echoing as if it's from another dimension.

2. **Clairvoyant (seeing images)**

   Clairvoyance is the intuitive ability to have a knowing about the future. If you are clairvoyant, you can also have the ability to gain information about a subject, location or even an object.

   Clairvoyants receive their messages from Source in many forms such as dreams, *dejavu*, images appearing in their minds eye and even experiencing strong feelings and vibrations from places and objects.

   Many experienced clairvoyants believe that the process is not specifically about mind reading but about feeling into the very heart and soul of the person they are engaged with. It is a gift to be able to see things that others cannot see.

3. **Clairsentience (recognising feelings)**

   Clairsentience is the intuitive ability to obtain knowledge from Source by sense or feeling and it is a deep knowing. Clairsentients often sense a person's physical and emotional pain, in the place on the body it occurred.

   Clairsentients have an absolute knowing of the energy that resides not just within themselves but also in that of others. They feel into the love that pulses from within our hearts and they feel into the thoughts, words and actions that are formed by this love.

   When you open your own heart and connect with it you can begin to switch on and into your own clairsentient essence. There is nothing more natural for you than feeling energy and you have been doing it since the day you were born.

4. **Claircognisance (knowing)**

   Claircognisance is the intuitive ability to obtain knowledge and insights from Source through wordless impressions that are in your mind and that your capacity to just 'know' something is strong within you.

   Claircognisance is also known as a 'clear-knowing', 'divine knowing', or 'drop-in insight'. Claircognisant information is often experienced like a light bulb being switched on suddenly in your head, or a sudden bright and clear idea.

   Claircognisant people can sense in their hearts that they know a particular piece of information that they have yet to be presented with and are consistently proven correct by the outcome of the situation despite having no information about the event.

HEARTING EXERCISE 1- WHAT IS YOUR PRIMARY PSYCHIC GIFT OR CLAIR?

Your intuition is a beautiful gift, and it is one that you currently possess whether you realise it or not. I encourage you not to be shy or intimidated about using your intuition and practice tuning in and really trusting yourself in this area.

I invite you to now answer a few questions to help you discover what your primary 'Clair' may be. Take a moment, close your eyes, breathe, and really feel into your heart and ground yourself in this moment. Now get your journal and answer the following questions:

GROUP 1

1. Do you frequently see things move out of the corner of your eye?
2. Do the lights flash on and off in your home sometimes for no apparent reason?
3. Do you frequently find coins?
4. When you have asked a question to Source do you often see names or numbers repeated in newspapers, online, billboards etc.

GROUP 2

1. Do you hear things on radio or television or online that answer questions you have thought about or contemplated to yourself?
2. Do you ever hear music that has no physical source?
3. Have you ever heard your name being called as you awaken to full consciousness after sleeping?
4. Do you ever experience a loud ringing in your ears?

GROUP 3

1. Do you dislike and avoid crowded situations?
2. Do you dislike conflict and arguments?
3. Do you dislike driving on crowded roads and heavy traffic?
4. Can you often tell what another person is feeling by the same feeling you are experiencing in your heart or gut?

GROUP 4

1. Have you ever known how to fix something electrical without any instructions or education or knowledge about the device?
2. Have you ever known who was on the telephone before you answered the call?
3. Has someone asked you a question and you have answered it without knowing how you know?

Now, I invite you to add up all of your 'Yes' responses for each of the groups.

How many Yes responses did you get in each group?

What group did you get the most yes responses?

This is your prime 'Clair'.

HEARTING EXERCISE 2 - FINE TUNING INTO YOUR CLAIR?

I invite you to now think about a beautiful holiday, or adventure, that you have been on that you loved, and really enjoyed yourself.

How would you describe this holiday or adventure to someone?

I invite you to write down what the four most important things you would want to share with someone about this amazing trip you experienced.

Why was it so amazing and enjoyable for you?

At the conclusion of the exercise, I invite you to consider if your memories were primarily about what you:

- saw
- felt
- heard
- smelt

I would note that whilst this exercise is certainly not definitive it will help guide you on your own personal journey to confirm your own primary 'Clair(s)' from which Source is communicating with you in your life.

Now what are you going to do with this information? How are you going to use it to your advantage and strengthen your connection with Source?

Please note, if you received a feeling or an insight during these exercises, this is not a coincidence, and you need to trust the messages you received and act upon them.

HEART ACTIVATION EXERCISES

I invite you to undertake the following four practices in your life daily:

1. Trust and surrender to your higher self and to Source
2. Open your consciousness to look outside of your own square and alter your perception of your reality
3. Recognise and be aware of your Ego and release negative and small beliefs that do not serve you
4. Learn humility in everything that you do

♥ Author's Heartnote: - I would highlight that when I refer to your inner child it also covers all your inner child(ren) from conception through to where you are right now.

47

HEARTING QUESTIONS

- *Are you connected to social media?*

- *Is your connection to social media keeping you disconnected from Source?*

- *Social media or Source – how much of your time in a normal day do you spend with each?*

INNER CHILD

Your inner child is your gateway to your higher self and to Source. In your journey of life, you are subjected to pains, hurts and traumatic events that impact upon you, and may wound your inner child.

It is an important part of your spiritual journey, and reconnecting with your heart, that you genuinely heal past wounds, retrieve your inner child from those wounds, reparent them and grow.

It is my experience that when people undertake the inner child journey they avoid reconnecting with certain painful and traumatic memories and the children associated and attached to these memories and feelings.

This approach may feel like it is keeping you safe, however by engaging sincerely and wholeheartedly with your inner child you will feel empowered; especially those that call out to you from their heart. If you ignore these inner children and their cries for help, it will be extremely challenging for you to connect with your heart and live into your best life.

When you undertake your inner child journey you may feel that your inner child is suddenly separate from You. It must be noted that this is not accurate, however for the point of the exercise there is a definite requirement for you to experience this 'perceived' separation. (In fact, this is how you know it is working.)

It has been my experience that people have felt a higher level of comfort once they have had this realisation. It is also important to note that the end goal here is for you to reach complete empowerment at which point your inner child (reaches your current age) and feels, safe, secure and as an integral part of you.

The journey with your inner child is unique and you may experience a degree of confusion and detachment whilst going through this process. I encourage you to take your time, reconnect, engage, and explore with a part of you that may have been seeking your love, attention, and forgiveness for years. Imagine a child left unattended, literally calling out for your attention to connect. Would you ignore them or take time to reconnect and heal with them?

How do you feel hearing this, what is coming up for you?

48

"May you always see the world through the eyes of a child"
C.S. LEWIS

"We don't stop playing because we grow old; we grow old because we stop playing"
GEORGE BERNARD SHAW

INNER CHILD WOUNDINGS

If you are unsure or unaware that you may have a wounded inner child here are some signs and indicators that this may be the case:

- You feel that there is something wrong with you, in the deepest parts of yourself
- You experience anxiety when venturing out of your comfort zone
- You are a people pleaser and avoid conflict
- You do not have a strong sense of personal identity
- You enjoy being in conflict with people around you
- You are a hoarder of things and have a hard time letting them go
- You feel you are not enough
- You distrust everyone, including yourself
- You constantly criticise yourself for your supposed inadequacies
- You are harsh and unforgiving on yourself'
- You are rigid and a perfectionist
- Your boundaries are either too weak or too rigid
- You have a very difficult time committing and trusting
- You have deep abandonment issues
- You cling to relationships even when they are toxic
- You were taught that it's not ok to have your own opinions
- You were punished when trying to speak up or act differently
- You were discouraged from being creative, playing or having fun
- You weren't allowed to be spontaneous
- You weren't allowed to show strong emotions such as anger or joy
- You were shamed by your parents or family members

"Loving your inner child helps you remember your innocence and recognise how much life loves you. Ask the child within, 'what can I do for you today?'"
UNKNOWN

- You were verbally criticized or abused on a regular basis
- You were physically punished by your parents or caregivers, e.g. smacked or beaten
- You were physically or sexually abused
- You were made to feel responsible for your parent's happiness
- You did not receive physical affection such as hugs, kisses or cuddles

These are just some of the signs that highlight that your inner child may be wounded and if any of these resonated with you then there is a high likelihood that you both need to spend quality time together to reconnect and heal.

How do you feel hearing this information?
What is coming up for you?

INNER CHILD CONNECTION BENEFITS

There are many beautiful benefits of reconnecting with your inner child and the most delightful and miraculous is that often your hidden gifts and talents will emerge after many years (and in some cases many decades) of being stifled. Reconnecting with your inner child also has significant second and third order benefits that will positively impact all areas of your life:

- you will have a stronger connection with your heart
- your relationships will improve
- your self-worth will improve
- your self-love will improve
- your friendships will improve
- your connection with yourself will deepen exponentially
- your creative self will flourish
- you will have a healthier mind, body, and soul

- addictions and self-destructive habits and patterns will start to lessen and disappear
- your ability to feel and express emotions such as acceptance, vulnerability, forgiveness, compassion and even love will improve

The benefits highlighted above are substantial and can be obtained when you choose to connect with your heart and undertake the inner child journey.

I invite you to connect with your inner child because when you are connected you will feel excited, invigorated, and inspired by life. When you are disconnected you will feel scared, fearful, tired, bored, unhappy and empty.

Please note that this is a relationship built on trust and it is crucial that you recognise the need for your inner child to trust you (your adult you). Also, note that just as important and often left out of consideration is your ability and requirement for You to trust in your own inner child and not be scared or fearful of them.

It is critical that you open your heart fully in your connection and trust that your inner child truly loves you and needs to reconnect and heal, that is why you two have come together.

Real food for heartfelt thought wouldn't you say?

How do you truly feel hearing this information?

What is coming up for you?

CONNECTING WITH YOUR INNER CHILD

There is a process to connect with your inner child and it should be done in a safe and secure environment.

Whilst I will provide you with the basic tools to help you through the process of connecting with your own inner child journeys, it is highly advisable that you action this process with professionals so that you get the best results.

"Hold the hand of the child that lives in your soul. For this child, nothing is impossible"
PAULO COELHO

"See the world through the eyes of your inner child. The eyes that sparkle in awe and amazement as they see love, magic, and mystery in the most ordinary things"
HENNA SOHAIL

"There is a child in all of us who continues to believe that it can always get better that it doesn't end here"
Vienna Pharaon

♥ **Author's Heartnote:** If possible, it is ideal to initially have a trained professional (Matrix Therapist/ Timeline Practitioner) support you when actioning this process to ensure your safety as well as ensuring that the key wounds are identified and healed appropriately.

There are eleven stages that I would like to take you through that relate to your inner child journey:

1. Put your hands on your heart and breathe

2. Close your eyes and remember that this is a safe and secure space and you and your inner child will be safe and protected at all times

3. Create your very own time machine that is going to take you back to see your inner child

4. Feel into your heart and listen and feel for your inner child who is calling out to you from a place associated with an event, thought or memory

5. Identifying and rediscovering your inner child (age, appearance, likes, dislikes, environment you find them in)

6. Create a relationship that forms trust between both of you.

7. Retrieval of your inner child – (You are seeking your inner child to come on the journey with you)

8. Reparenting your inner child – (You are communicating directly with them)

9. Growing with your inner child – (You are holding space and watching them grow and develop and inviting them to join you on your life journey)

10. Rinse and repeat – (at each new age encountered until you reach your current age, then move onto stage 7)

11. The amalgamation of your inner child with yourself - True Spiritual empowerment is achieved once you amalgamate all your ages into your current age and you do this by … embracing your child as whole and an inseparable part of YOU. (You will know this has been achieved because everything in your life from this point forward will have changed for the better. Just be reminded that you will still need to connect with Source and Heart.)

HEART ACTIVATION EXERCISE 1 - FUN WAYS TO START TO RECONNECT WITH YOUR INNER CHILD

1. Find a photo of your younger self and put it in your wallet or your phone. *When you start to engage in negative and destructive self-talk find your photo and attempt to have the same conversation with your younger self.*

2. Create a compassionate dialogue with your inner child. *Perhaps as part of your heart and soul trysts. Remind yourself that this is not a tryst with your adult self but a tryst with your younger self!*

3. Start to have loving heartfelt conversations with your inner child and be compassionate and nurturing by telling your inner child that you love them, you hear them, you thank them. You could even apologise and seek forgiveness if your heart truly desires for this to be done.

4. Ask your inner child what they love to do.

5. Laugh with your inner child.

6. Take time for yourself and your inner child and engage in meditation and creative visualisation.

HEART ACTIVATION EXERCISE 2 – HURTS, PAINS AND TRAUMA

What three events have significantly impacted your life and your heart?

1.

2.

3.

Have you come to terms with these events?

Have you healed from all these events?

What are three positive steps you are going to take to start to heal from your unhealed hurts, pains, and traumas?

Over the past month what feelings have you noticed in your heart?

What heart connected feelings would you like to experience more of on a regular basis?

What are three actions you will commit to now that will empower you to experience the heartfelt feelings you want on a regular basis?

1.

2.

3.

HEARTING QUESTIONS

- *When was the last time you truly connected with your inner child?*

- *How often do you take the time to tune in and listen to the needs of your inner child?*

Do you regularly make time to connect, play and enjoy life with your inner child? Your Heart Trysts and Heart Whispers are powerful tools that directly link you with your inner child. They are the cornerstones for connection to your soul.

- *Do you have any resistance to getting to know your inner child? If so, I invite you to gift yourself permission to delve a little deeper and ask yourself (your adult) Why?*

- *What did you do with your inner child when you connected?*

- *If you have not connected with your inner child recently, what do you believe your inner child would like to do with you?*

- *What would your inner child say to you right now if they were standing in front of you?*

HEART (COMPASSIONATE MIND)

I believe that people have lost their ability to make a direct connection with their heart. In the world today people like to talk about how they are 'heart centered' and 'heart based'. They tell you that to live with heart is important to living a great full life.

Companies, organisations, and government departments have all jumped on the 'heart' bandwagon as though it is a panacea that will erase decades of bullying, neglect, and mistreatment of people at all levels.

It has become trendy to be 'heart centered' and 'heart based' or to call yourself 'heart centered' and 'heart based'. However, like all things, there is a process that needs to be taken to actually connect with and activate your heart. It is a conscious and spiritually awakening process, and it takes courage to step into your heart space to locate and reactivate your heart, let alone discover your Hidden Heart!

"It's impossible, said pride. It's risky, said experience. It's pointless, said reason. Give it a try, whispered the heart"
UNKNOWN

"If you don't follow your heart, you might spend the rest of your life wishing you had"
BRIGITTE NICOLE

"Your heart knows things that your mind can't explain"
UNKNOWN

There have been many cultures that have interconnected the significance of individual spiritual practice with the importance of being guided and following your heart. When you follow your heart, you gain wisdom and intelligence in everything you do and everything you are. Again, I make the point that when I refer to your heart in this Book, I am not just referring to your physical beating organ but to your spiritual heart as well.

Also, just as your brain is an organ and viewed as having a consciousness and a 'mind of its own', your spiritual heart has a level of consciousness all its own as well. Your heart not only has a spiritual level of consciousness, from a purely neurological perspective your heart is also a brain, and it has a unique language that it uses to communicate with you all the time.

Are you aware that your heart is a brain that communicates directly with you?

What do you feel your heart brain is saying to you right now?

Your heart is the key to your own self-actualization, inner peace, and fulfillment. Your heart is the doorway to experiencing a truly deeper relationship with Source and self that is characterised by profound compassion, joy, peace, safety, and unconditional love.

WHAT IS THE SCIENTIFIC DEFINITION OF YOUR HEART?

Your heart is a vital organ. It is a muscle that pumps blood to every part of your body, and it provides your body with the oxygen and nutrients it needs to function.

The four main functions of the heart are:

- Pumping oxygenated blood to the other body parts
- Pumping hormones and other vital substances to different parts of the body
- Receiving deoxygenated blood and carrying metabolic waste products from the body and pumping it to the lungs for oxygenation

- Maintaining blood pressure

FUN FACTS ABOUT YOUR HEART

Your heart:
- is the size of an adult fist
- weighs between 300 and 450 grams
- has four chambers (just like your Hidden Heart Diamond has four parts)
- beats about 115,000 times every day
- pumps about 7,570 litres (2,000 gallons) of blood every day
- has an electrical system that controls its rhythm
- can continue beating even when it's disconnected from your body

WHAT IS THE METAPHYSICAL AND SPIRITUAL DEFINITION OF YOUR HEART?

Your heart's highest expression is compassion, it is your affectional consciousness and is your direct conduit, or link, to Source. Your heart is the spiritual gateway by which Source communicates with and through you and is the centre from which your spiritual energy emanates.

Your heart symbolizes the center or 'core' of your very being, it is the control center from which prayer, meditation and your moral actions originate. This even explains the word "core," which is derived from the Latin word (spelt cor), meaning, 'heart.'

Your heart is your compassionate mind. It is truth. Your physical heart supplies blood to your body and your spiritual heart feeds and nourishes your soul (from Source) and is the very essence of who you are; a spiritual being having the human experience.

"You will never be able to escape from your heart, so it is better to listen to what it has to say"
PAOLO COEHLO

"Be bold enough to use your voice, brave enough to listen to your heart and strong enough to live the life you have always wanted"
UNKNOWN

WHAT IS *m*BRAINING PERSPECTIVE OF YOUR HEART?

Your heart is a brain and operates as a brain with somewhere between 40,000 and 120,000 neurons. Your heart communicates with your other brains (head, gut, ANS and pelvic) and is a complex, powerful intelligence.

Your heart has a different way of processing, communicating, operating, and addressing issues and problems you encounter in the world from your head and your gut.

The highest expression of your heart brain is 'Compassion', and its prime functions relate to 'emoting', 'relational affects' and 'values'. Your heart is much more than a bodily organ pumping blood around your body!

HEART BASED LANGUAGE (IDIOMS AND SAYINGS)

Are you aware that you have been using neuro linguistics to communicate from your heart (and your other brains)? Your heart has meaning and permanence outside of your physical body. You use it in everyday language to express your feelings and emotions and you may not even be aware of it!

1. **Eat your heart out** – to express strong (negative) emotions such as jealousy, grief, anguish
2. **From the bottom of my heart** – with utmost sincerity (and usually regret)
3. **Have a heart** – "Show some pity!", "Try and be sympathetic!"
4. **Heart and soul** – energy, enthusiasm
5. **In a heartbeat** – immediately
6. **My heart bleeds for/goes out to…** – "I feel very sorry for/sympathetic towards…"
7. **To find it in your heart to do something** – to summon up willingness to do something

8. **To follow your heart** – to act according to your emotions and desires

9. **To get to the heart of something** – to understand the central, most essential aspect of something

10. **To have a change of heart** – to change your mind

11. **To have a heart of gold/stone** – to be generous and kind/cold and cruel

12. **To have a heart to heart** – to have an intimate conversation

13. **To have your heart miss/skip a beat** – to be startled or surprised

14. **To have your heart in the right place** – to be well intentioned

15. **To have your heart set against something** – to be against something

16. **To have your heart set on something** – to want something very much

17. **To know in your heart of hearts** – to know something as true despite not wanting to believe it

18. **To know/learn something off by heart** – to know something from memory

19. **To lose heart** – to give up, to feel discouraged, to lose hope

20. **To not have your heart in something** – to not really want to do something

21. **To pour your heart out** – to vent your feelings

22. **To take something to heart** – to take something seriously (and usually with offence)

23. **To tug at someone's heartstrings** – to appeal to someone's emotions, make them feel sad or guilty

24. **To wear your heart on your sleeve** – to openly express your feelings

25. **With a heavy heart** – with sorrow and regret

These common everyday expressions clearly indicate that from a neuro linguistic perspective that intelligence, intuition, and wisdom are taking place in your heart space and your heart is communicating with you every moment of every day. This is a very powerful realisation to consider and reflect upon.

HEART AS YOUR FOURTH CHAKRA

An important aspect of your personal journey is to discover that your heart is more than just a physical organ, it plays a significant role in guiding and balancing your mental, emotional, and spiritual self. A deeper understanding of your heart will benefit you in every part of your life and enable you to live into your best life.

Your heart chakra, known in Sanskrit as Anahata, is the fourth chakra and is in the center of your chest it is not located where your actual heart organ is. It is the point that balances your lower chakras (human and Ego) and your higher chakras (light and Source), and it is the doorway to your soul and Source. Connecting and activating your heart and your heart chakra is a powerful way to integrate the higher and lower selves and the light and the dark within you.

It is through your heart chakra where you will learn to understand and accept your darkness, limitations, failings and your hurt, pain, and fear. When you learn to embrace and love these aspects of yourself you start on your journey towards the light and something far greater than your Ego.

Your heart chakra is the primary chakra associated with the element of air and its energy is associated with your breath and the movement and flow of your breath, as well as your awareness of space and your connection with all things. It is also associated with green and in higher energy frequencies, it can turn to pink. I would like you to note that the key functions associated with your heart chakra are:

60

"There is a light that shines beyond the world, beyond everything, beyond all, beyond the highest heaven. This is the light that shines within your heart."
UPANISHADS

"As you live deeper in the heart, the mirror gets cleaner and cleaner"
RUMI

- Love for yourself and others
- Relationships and connecting with yourself and others
- Compassion and empathy for yourself and others
- Acceptance and forgiveness for yourself and others
- Transformation and change
- Your ability to grieve and reach peace after grieving
- Sensitivity and judgement in all situations
- Awareness and intuition

When your heart chakra is open, you will feel connected to the harmonious exchange of energy of the Universe and with all that is around you, as well as having a deep appreciation of beauty.

Your heart chakra is not always open and can also become imbalanced and blocked because of life experiences that have a traumatic event attached to them and which you store in your heart space. The signs of these imbalances and blockages manifest in the following ways in your life, especially in relation to your interactions with others:

- Being over defensive
- Feeling closed down and withdrawn
- Feeling shy and lonely
- Being excessively jealous
- Having a fear of intimacy
- Being codependent and relying on other's approval and attention
- Trying to please at all cost
- Having harsh judgement of yourself and others
- Lacking empathy for self and others
- Being the savior or the rescuer; or being the victim
- Existing in excessive isolation, being reclusive and antisocial
- Holding grudges and not being able to forgive

"Don't be pushed around by the fears in your mind. Be led by the dreams in your heart"
ROY T. BENNETT

At the physical level, an imbalanced or blocked heart chakra can manifest as:

- Respiratory ailments, such as lung infection and bronchitis
- Circulatory and heart-related issues

When the energy flow in your fourth chakra is blocked or out of balance, you may experience what is sometimes referred to as heart chakra pain.

If you feel that your heart chakra may be out of balance or blocked it is primarily because you are holding onto, and storing, these repressed emotions in your heart space.

When you repress traumatic emotions such as those mentioned, it can take you out of flow on your life path and energetically move you out of sync with living your life's true purpose. The saddest part of this is that you may know and be aware of what is going on but feel powerless to do anything about it.

How do you feel hearing this?

What is coming up for you?

HEART ACTIVATION EXERCISE

I invite you to now set these three intentions to deal with any of your repressed emotions, whether you are consciously aware of them or not:

1. Be fully open and present with your feelings and emotions any way you desire! You can write them down via your Heart Whispers or you can scream them out loud to the Universe. It does not matter what way you feel you need to release these feelings and emotions; they need to be released for you and for your heart. When

you are releasing these feelings and emotions, I invite you to be open and honest with everything you have repressed, do not hold anything back.

2. Stop living your life through past pains, hurts and traumas. It is a choice that you are making every time you do so. When you choose to live in these past states of emotion, they drain your life energy and block your heart from living into its highest expression of compassion. Your own personal journeys to reconnect and reparent your inner child and deal with past traumas and emotions will significantly benefit you in this regard and should be undertaken when necessary.

3. Practice the art of acceptance and gratitude. Gratitude is a powerful way for you to appreciate what you have instead of living into a life of what you do not. In the research on positive psychology, it has been shown that gratitude is heavily and consistently associated with greater happiness. When you truly practice gratitude, it will enhance your life experiences and improve your health and help you deal with adversity and live a better life.

I invite you to incorporate these three intentions into your daily life and I gently remind you that love is your greatest healer and that love, and compassion come from your heart – This is not an accident!

Again, the choice is yours.

What do you plan to do about it?

I invite you to consider using affirmations as they are a powerful way of removing old and limiting beliefs and for building confidence. Your heart chakra will directly respond to affirmations when you use certain words and phrases.

You should say them at least once every day and be saying them as often as you need to. It is also a good idea to alter or change your affirmations over time to ensure your heart chakra is being stimulated, unblocked, and healed.

If you feel you need to repeat certain affirmations, then feel into what your heart chakra desires and say them. Here are some examples for you to use with your heart chakra:

- I choose compassion, joy and love
- Every day, I make sure I fulfill my heart's desire
- I know my own emotions, and fully accept whatever form they may be
- I am fully open to love and to receive more love every day
- I give love freely and generously and it brings me great joy
- My heart chakra is always open and I am great
- I create supportive, loving and nurturing relationships that are good for me
- I forgive others and I forgive myself
- I love myself unconditionally and offer that same love to others
- My heart is free from all the wounds of my past

64

"Your diet is a bank account. Good food choices are good investments"
BETHANY FRANKEL

"In a crystal we have clear evidence of the existence of a formative life principle, and though we cannot understand the life of a crystal, it is nonetheless a living being"
NIKOLA TESLA

HEART - FOURTH CHAKRA HEALING FOODS

Just as each chakra has its own vibrational frequency, color, and purpose, they also have foods that help strengthen and empower individual chakra functions. In relation to your heart chakra, I invite you to consider adding naturally green-colored foods such as, spinach, zucchini, kale, broccoli, avocado, cucumbers, asparagus, peas, beans, brussels sprouts, kiwi fruit, green apples, green grapes and limes.

I invite you to consider the following green super foods, spirulina, chlorella, wheatgrass, barley grass, matcha powder, and green tea are all another source for healing your fourth chakra. Herbs such as coriander, mint, oregano, parsley, thyme, rosemary, tarragon, basil, and sage are another source of healing.

Your heart chakra is critical to you connecting to Source, and these foods should become part of your diet on a regular basis. So what action, if any, are you going to consider incorporating these foods into your life?

HEART - FOURTH CHAKRA HEALING STONES

Your heart chakra is also activated and can be healed by specific healing stones. Crystals such as emerald; green aventurine; jade; malachite; green calcite; chrysoprase; green and pink tourmaline; rose quartz and kunzite can have a very powerful effect and influence over your heart chakra. I invite you to feel into your heart space and ask your heart what crystal(s) it truly wants to connect with.

These crystals can be incorporated into your life and used to bring you into deeper connection, healing, and growth.

HEARTING EXERCISES

1. Gift yourself time and permission to do your balanced heart breathing on a regular basis
2. Encourage yourself and grow your appreciation for beauty, whether it is in nature, people, or the arts
3. Practice self-care and love your body; try a bath with rose essential oils

4. Cultivate self-compassion and acceptance, especially with regards to your body and emotions

5. Engage in activities that feed your heart

6. Focus on receiving if you are naturally inclined to be a giver, and on giving if you're more inclined to receive all the time. Here are some hearting questions for you to consider:

   a. Why do I love to give so much? Why do you feel it is easier to be a giver than to receive? What comes up for you about receiving?

   b. Why do I love to receive so much? Why do you feel it is easier to be a receiver than to be a giver? What comes up for you about giving?

7. Be courageous and heal old hurts, pains and traumas with compassion and love and practice forgiveness deep within your heart

8. Express your gratitude. You can be grateful for the presence of other people in your life or simply for good things that make your life easier and happier

---

HEARTING QUESTIONS

- *What is your heart to You?*

- *Where is your heart in your life?*

- *On a scale of 1 to 11, 1 being not at all and 11*

being all the time, how often do you truly feel into your heart when making decisions and living your life daily?

Are you truly connected to your heart? Give 5 examples of why you are and why you are not.

1.

2.

3.

4.

5.

What are 3 things you are going to do, in the next week, to truly feel into your heart and live into your best life?

1.

2.

3.

"*If you have a strong purpose in life, you don't have to be pushed. Your passion will drive you there*"
ROY T. BENNETT

"*The best day of your life is the one on which you decide your life is your own. No apologies or excuses. No one to lean on, rely on or blame. The gift is yours; it is an amazing journey, and you alone are responsible for the quality of it. This is the day your life really begins*"
BOB MOAWAD

"*The greatest tragedy in life isn't death, but a life without a purpose*"
MYLES MUNROE

"*You can't do anything about the length of your life, but you can do something about its width and depth*"
H. L. MENCKEN

LIFE PURPOSE

Your Hidden Heart Diamond consists of elements comprising Source, inner child, heart (compassionate mind) and is the framework in which your hidden heart is located.

When you are connected with Source, your inner child and heart your life purpose begins to emerge because you are in alignment with who you know you truly are. It is a deep knowing and it forms an energy within you and allows for your life to flow seamlessly.

When you are not in flow and not connected to one of your elements then all are affected, and you will feel a sense of disconnection from the world at large and from your life purpose in general. It is a deep spiritual knowing and you feel it in your heart.

On your hidden heart journey, you have been travelling on the path that you have created and designed for you. It is uniquely yours and only you know what it has been and whether you are truly living into your best life, including your life purpose.

I invite you to feel into your heart and consider the following statements as a foundation you can embrace to help you discover your life purpose:

- I do everything in my power to discover my life's purpose
- I am discovering my life's purpose and creating positive changes to my life every day
- My life's purpose empowers me to shape my own destiny

YOUR LIFE VALUES AND LIVING YOUR LIFE PURPOSE

Your life values are significant and important indicators to help guide you to your life purpose. Your values serve as markers on your life journey to keep you on your true path throughout your entire life.

Your life values define you and who you are. They are intangible and whilst they may be challenging to quantify it is very important that you feel into your heart and learn to identify and know what they are, because they are you.

Your life values are not what you do, although they can be reflected in how you do it. For example, someone who is buying a car may have a value of beauty and buy a red Porsche sports car because it is aesthetically pleasing to them. Someone else may have a value of safety and buy a Jeep or a Land Rover because it is strong and sturdy. Both people bought cars, however it was why they did it that reflected their own life values.

Your life values are a part of your DNA, and when you live into your life values through your heart, you become connected with who you were created to be. I invite you to consider that your life values are not:

- **Principles** – are rules based and are attached to philosophies, ideologies, ethics, and doctrines. If you are following rules, then you are following the principles embedded in these rules and not your core life values.

- **Needs** – are what you think you require for you to live a full, happy life. They reflect your desires and your wishes. If you must have something or somebody to live a happy full life, then that is a need. You do not need a life value; you already have all of them within you.

- **Emotions** – are what you feel. Your emotional states are not your life values. Your values will remain predominately fixed or constant whereas your emotions can change rapidly and are influenced by your personal perceptions of events in your life.

- **Beliefs** – are your personal collection of life experiences. Values are not life experiences. As you grow you are subjected to many competing forces and ideas, and you make your own judgments about what you experienced. Is it 'good', is it 'bad', am I 'right', am I 'wrong', is it 'legal', is it 'illegal', is it 'ethical', is it 'unethical'? Your belief list is endless. Your beliefs are outside influences from parents, brothers and sisters, teachers, friends, partners. Your life values come from within you.

♥ **Author's Heartnote:** I would like to guide you towards Part IV – Hidden Heart Learnings of the Book where you will find valuable information about discovering your values and your shadow values and I invite you to explore and complete those sections.

- **Morals** – give you a feeling of being righteous or ethical about yourself and aspects of your life. If you feel righteous or ethical about what you are doing, this is not a life value it is a moral. Morals are laws and regulations either written or implied that set boundaries of behaviour by which you then act and live in a certain way.

- **Should's** – do not come easily and usually feel forced. A should or a should not, is not your voice. Just like morals, beliefs, and principles, a should is an external influence upon you. A should is somebody else's voice telling you what they want you to do. When you live into a 'should', just how old is that voice you are hearing and whose voice is it? Is it your inner child still trying to be good and do the right thing and doing what it 'should' be doing? When you 'should' you are setting up an internal resistance and conflict within you. A should has nothing to do with your current reality, so take a moment the next time you should or should not do something and see where that voice is coming from.

"Decisions are the hardest thing to make, especially when it is a choice between where you should be and where you want to be"
UNKNOWN

"One day your life will flash before your eyes, make sure it's worth watching"
GERARD WAY

When you have difficulty making important decisions in your life it is primarily because you are not following your heart and are not following your life values. You know when you 'make a decision' if it is in sync with your heart and your life values as it is a deep knowing.

When you make a choice that is not in alignment your life will become more difficult and you feel it, it is palpable. When you feel like you have lost control of your life or have very little control this is what happens. You have a choice to honor your life values or not. So, what is your choice?

Once you identify your most important life values your decision making and life choices will become easier and there will be a flow and symmetry to everything you do.

Your life choices will become easier because you will know who you are and why you are and because of this you will have a much better quality of life.

Who do you feel you are?

Your values influence what you do and the decisions you make. Values are the principles that give your life meaning.

To live an empowered and transformed life it is important that you have a deeper understanding of what your core values are.

Your core values are the fundamental beliefs that you use to live your life. They are your guiding principles by which you view the world.

When you live into your values you are connecting with your heart and making a commitment to be true to who you are.

I invite you to go to the Heart Learning Exercise related to your values and feel into the experience.

THE ESSENCE OF YOUR VALUES

Your values are important in helping you unlock and discover what your true purpose is however they are not the definitive guide.

I invite you to consider that what is also critical is the importance of obtaining the essence of your life purpose. Your values provide you with the foundation of the pathway on which your life purpose exists and discovering the essences of that purpose helps refine it even further.

Your life purpose essences provide you with the tools, knowledge and understanding to have the power to:

- Highlight the key elements that already exist in your life
- Make informed, heartfelt decisions and choices that are in alignment with your life purpose

When you journey to discover the essence of your values there are threshold exercises and questions that must be completed for you to gain a clearer understanding and appreciation of what they truly are.

HEART PLANNING YOUR VALUES ESSENCE

The first exercise I invite you to complete in distilling your essence of your values is a Heart Plan (it is a mind map for your heart!). A Heart Plan is a beautiful and powerful tool that will provide you with greater clarity about your life purpose and it is a lot of fun to create.

Heart Plan Example

To start your heart plan, draw a heart on a large sheet of paper and place the words 'life purpose' in the middle of it. Now feel into your heart and ask it what it wants and desires to tell you and when words or images manifest you will write them down or draw them on your plan and draw a line from the heart to the word or image.

As words and images start to manifest you just keep writing them down and drawing them where you feel is appropriate. Each new line that comes out from the center of your heart plan is a new branch that is describing a different part of who you are.

I invite you to set yourself a time limit to complete your heart plan and do not worry about spelling or the appearance of how it looks on the page. What is important is what you have written down and drawn! Do not listen to your Ego or your head but follow your heart and allow yourself to explore your passions, interests, likes, dislikes, and all the many beautiful things in your life that provide you with a deeper understanding of who you truly are.

When you have completed your heart plan it is important to observe what you have written and drawn objectively. Stand back and look at your page and see what really stands out for you.

What do you notice most about it?

Are there any surprises?

Get yourself a highlighter pen and circle or highlight anything that is important, stands out or you repeated.

Are there any of your life values represented in your Heart Plan?

If you drew images, how big are they on the page?

Are they detailed?

What color are they?

When you reflect on your Heart Plan it is important to understand that whatever comes up for you is only a reflection of where you are right now, and you can change it if you choose to.

You may feel that you are not important enough or that you have missed opportunities and are unsure of who you are. These feelings and emotions are all part of your journey and will help you to go deeper, heal and grow.

I now invite you to uncover aspects of your plan that may not be present in what you wrote down. Take out your journal and make a list of five areas of your life that consume most of your time.

Now make a list of five things you love and five things you don't love about what consumes your time. Now give them a rating out of eleven of how energised each makes you feel. These lists will provide you with important information about how you are currently living into your life.

The information you have been collecting related to your core values and your heart plan will resonate within you, and it is important to look at what you have written and truly feel into

"An empowered life begins with serious personal questions about oneself. Those answers bare the seeds of success"
STEVE MARSHALL

"Accept no one's definition of your life; define yourself"
HARVEY FIERSTEIN

73

what three life values must be honoured, without exception, in your life? Also, what are the three most important things that you must have in your life to feel fulfilled?

1.

2.

3.

74

"A bad day for your Ego is a great day for your soul"
JILLIAN MICHAELS

"Ego is just like dust in your eyes. Without clearing the dust, you cannot see clearly. So, clear the Ego and see the world"
UNKNOWN

"Ego – three letters that hold you back from saying things your heart is dying to say like, I love you, I miss you and I am sorry"
UNKNOWN

"The Ego seeks to divide and separate. Spirit seeks to unify and heal"
PEMA CHODRON

These six value essences will provide you with a clearer understanding and a deeper appreciation and knowing about what is truly important to you at a heart level in your life. I encourage you to take note of what they are and embrace them for in doing so you will be embracing yourself at a deep level.

HEARTING QUESTIONS

• *If you were financially wealthy, how would you spend your time?*

What would your perfect day look and feel like? (Get a 24-hour diary page (*create your own*) and schedule your perfect day and leave nothing out.)

• *What do you do that sets your heart and soul on fire?*

• *What is your heart telling you?*

EGO

I invite you to start by feeling into a beautiful quote from Eckhart Tolle:

"Give up defining yourself – to yourself or to others. You won't die. You will come to life. And don't be concerned with how others define you. When they define you, they are limiting themselves, so it's their problem. Whenever you interact with people, don't be there primarily as a function or a role, but as the field of conscious Presence. You can only lose something that you have, but you cannot lose something that you are." Eckhart Tolle, A New Earth

The New Oxford American Dictionary defines Ego as, '*the part of the mind that mediates between the conscious and the unconscious and is responsible for reality testing and a sense of personal identity*'. The word Ego originates from the early 19th century Latin and translates directly to 'I' and is synonymous with Sigmund Freud's theory on the human psyche.

The Ego, the Id and the Super Ego became part of the lexicon of modern times and whilst there have been a multitude of books, scholarly articles and scientific studies that have been undertaken on the Ego and its iterations. In the Book the focus is on your Ego from a metaphysical and heart-based perspective. If you want a deeper psychological understanding for yourself, then I invite you to undertake your own study and find out more.

Everyone has an Ego, and your Ego can be a positive force in your life. Your ego helps you survive and protects your self-image and self-worth. However, your Ego can also keep you small and can cost you dearly in fulfilling your life's purpose and living into your best life.

Your Ego can become your biggest enemy and keep you disconnected from reality and what is happening in the world around you. Your Ego also prevents you from hearing and receiving critical and constructive feedback from others. When you leave your Ego unchecked it can also overestimate and inflate your own abilities and worth and underestimate the level of effort, knowledge and skill required to set and achieve goals.

In this Book the focus in relation to your Ego is not to analyse what your Ego is or is not. The focus is on the impact your Ego has on your heart and your life, including its power to derail your life flow and disconnect you from Source, heart, inner child, life purpose and your hidden heart.

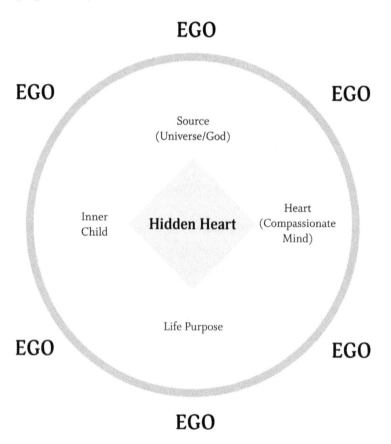

In the process of disconnecting, you form Source, heart, inner child and life purpose, your Ego can also totally disrupt and disconnect you from your hidden heart. Your Ego operates outside of your Hidden Heart Diamond and whilst it may operate outside of your Diamond it manifests to take you out of flow and alignment and has the capacity to keep you on your own 'hamster wheel' of life and strip the compassion, joy, and fun out of everything you do.

When you accept that your Ego will always be a part of your life and not taking up residency in you, you will recognise that you have the authority, power and control to develop your Ego so that it has a level of integrity and you can start to integrate your Ego with your heart in a way that will enhance your life beyond measure.

When you hearten your life, it is important that your focus is beyond the material aspects of your existence. When you feel into your life beyond the material, your concept of who you are and what you are capable of will expand exponentially.

When you live your life from this perspective you will realise that what makes you unique isn't the thoughts you have about yourself driven from your Ego, but instead it is an expansive awareness that is centered around compassion, and this is what plays witness to your inner world and your inner being.

I invite you to now consider and feel into the concept that your world and your Universe and everything in it is interconnected. You are a part of a collective that interacts with every other and that your Ego has the potential for programming, both positive and negative with you as its master. Your interaction with your Ego can have a substantial impact on how you perceive yourself and the world.

It is important to note that if you leave your Ego unchecked your self-image can focus on the self and create the illusion that you are alone and just a solitary being disconnected from your heart and your spiritual self. When you choose to live your life through your Ego, it is important to recognise that it is solely focused on a material existence, short-term self-gratification, and survival.

"You need a large Ego for as long as you are ignorant of your larger sense of SELF"
CHRIS W. METZ

77

Living an Ego led life is hollow, and leaves you feeling anxious, fearful, and small as it makes you believe that you are nothing more than one person, one body, one mind and one heart when in fact the opposite is the case.

You are a part of a vast interconnected Universe that is joined on a myriad of levels and dimensions, and it is your heart that literally beats the energy necessary to be a part of it.

HEARTING QUESTIONS

Right here, right now, ask yourself these questions:

- *Am I the person I always wanted to be, living into my best life, being everything, I always dreamed of?*

- *How much has your Ego cost you?*

- *How much will it cost you and your life in the future?*

- *The choice is yours!*

- *So, what are you going to do?*

- *What life are you going to choose?*

- *Are you going to access the collective via your interconnected universe or live through your Ego?*

HEARTING EXERCISE – YOUR EGO TABLE

I invite you to draw a table with two columns and in the left column and title it 'Ego' and in the right column I invite you to title it 'Source/Heart/Inner Child'.

Now under Ego I invite you to list the following Ego specific characteristics. Please feel free to add to the list with other characteristics that are specific to you:

EGO	SOURCE/ HEART/ INNER CHILD
Fear	Unconcern
Depression	Joy
Anxiety	Calmness
Worry	Composed
Arrogance	Humility
Regret	Contentment
Dissatisfaction	Self-satisfaction
Pomposity	Modesty
Vanity	Humility
Pride	Humility
Anger	Calm
Jealousy	Trust
Hate	Love
Restriction	Freedom
Despair	Hope
Meanness	Generosity
Fantasy	Reality
Indifference	Passion

This is not an exhaustive list, but it has been designed to provide you with a clear understanding of what your Ego is about and the role it has played in your life.

HEARTING EXERCISE - GUIDING YOUR EGO

Your Ego is attached to your human experience and is not attached in any way to your spiritual self or your heart. The only bridge is when you relate feelings to specific emotional woundings and traumatic events.

It is important to understand this because when you operate from your heart and view traumatic events and associated feelings with true compassion, you can dismantle the bridge between Ego and spirit allowing for healing, spiritual awakening, and growth to take place.

Everything starts and ends with your heart. When you introduce your heart to Ego, it (your heart) becomes a powerful force that will keep you grounded and heart centered and will stop you spinning out of control, especially on an emotional and spiritual level.

Guide 1 – I invite you to imagine your Ego is a tiny monkey on your shoulder whispering in your ear and warning you of every possible negative outcome that may occur if you take a particular course of action or 'make a decision' on something in your life.

For example, the first time you asked someone out on a date, what did you feel?

What happened with your ego when you were considering taking action?

When you leave your little monkey unattended it can grow and turn into King Kong. A beast whose sole purpose is to cripple you with a range of feelings

80   *"The Ego is like a clever monkey, which can co-opt anything, even the most spiritual practices, to expand itself"*
JEAN YVES LELOUP

and emotions including fear, doubt, confusion, guilt, anger, resistance and create walls and story that do not serve you in any way.

When your King Kong Ego takes control, your heart is literally shut down and frozen out of any meaningful role or relationship with yourself or others. There is a seismic disconnection with every element of your Hidden Heart Diamond.

The key to disarming your King Kong Ego is to develop strategies to dimmish its importance and power over your heart and life.

1. Recognising when your little monkey is starting to grow into a killer ape
2. Balanced breathing to help reset and align with the Hidden Heart Diamond
3. Realising that you are always in control and always empowered to make the final decision on your own life, including your Ego

Guide 2 – Imagine your Ego as a separate entity with a name. Give it form and substance and name it. In naming your Ego you are forming a connection that your heart can feel into and have compassion for. Your heart can begin to love this new entity and disarm it so that you can live into your best life with empowerment, freedom, and purpose.

For example, Nicole named her ego 'Elsa'. Elsa was out of control and played havoc in Nicole's life and kept Nicole small and very safe. Nicole was an accomplished corporate professional; however her Ego had a massive negative impact on how she saw herself and functioned in every area of her life.

When Nicole started to recognise her Ego, and after naming it, she was able to acknowledge, accept and love it. Nicole would speak with Elsa when she felt Elsa stirring and rising. She would tell Elsa that she was loved and appreciated and the fact that she was trying to protect her and that whilst this was a positive thing it was Nicole who was now in control of making decisions and living her own life and not her Ego Elsa.

Nicole has transformed her life in all areas and admits that she is unrecognisable from the woman she had been. Nicole also found that by using humor, wit, and cheekiness that her Ego has diminished and no longer has the dominance and control it once did.

Nicole is now in control of the interactions and feels more empowered and connected to her heart and is living into her best life and building her spiritual muscle day by day.

HEARTING EXERCISE – METAPHYSICAL EGO IDENTIFICATION

It is important to note that prior to engaging with your inner child or seeking to obtain a true heart connection you need to identify your Ego. This exercise is a very gentle way to help you understand a little bit more on a metaphysical level, of what your Ego is manifesting as in your life. There is a metaphysical Ego disconnection that is not a part of this Book but is a very powerful process to spiritually disconnect Ego from you.

When you look at your Hidden Heart Diamond the Ego is present, however it sits outside of the four

82

"I can respect any person who can put their Ego aside and say, I made a mistake, 'I apologise, and I am correcting my behavior'"
SYLVESTER MCNUTT III

elements and whilst it appears as though it doesn't have a big effect on what is happening in your life, nothing could be further from the truth.

Your Ego will bypass every element of your Hidden Heart Diamond and disconnect you from all of it, and that is why it is imperative that it is disconnected so you can manage it.

You cannot remove your Ego completely, but it is important that its dominance is reduced in your life and here is a framework you can use to help you:

1. Close your eyes and breathe into your thoughts and feelings around your Ego
2. Invite your intuition to help you identify Ego from your beautiful mind?
3. Describe your Ego – Name, form, shape, color, energy (recognise it)
4. Where is it in relation to you? (Inside you or outside you?)
5. Now feel into your heart and ask Source to verify if what is presenting is your Ego (you may be surprised!)
6. If it is inside you then gently remove it and place it in front of you
7. Imagine your Ego's energy starting to deplete and get smaller
8. Have a conversation with your Ego as it is in front of you and let it know that it is loved and that You are going to be stepping up and taking control back of your life. Let your Ego know that You are in the driver seat now

HEARTING QUESTIONS

I invite you to recognise the impact your Ego has had on you. The decisions you have and have not made because of your Ego.

- *How are you feeling about your Ego and the impact it has had on your life?*

- *Can you feel the direct link that your Ego has always had in your life? (Destructive? Go into detail about the negative impacts it has had on your life.) Where is your Ego in your life now?*

- *How would you describe your Ego now?*

- *What degree of influence does your Ego have in your life?*

Over the past four weeks when did you recognise your Ego rising and controlling you? Give three examples.

1.

2.

3.

What are five things your Ego is stopping you from doing (now)?

1.

2.

3.

4.

5.

PART IV

HIDDEN HEART
LEARNINGS

88

"A lack of boundaries invites a lack of respect"
UNKNOWN

"Boundaries: By definition, a boundary is anything that marks a limit. Psychological limits define personal dignity. When we say, 'You just crossed a line', we are speaking about a psychological limit that marks the distinction between behavior that does not cause emotional harm and behavior that causes emotional harm"
UNKNOWN

In your Hidden Heart journey, the quintessential element revolves around you choosing to connect with your heart and live into your best compassionate life.

The catch cry of this Book is that *'everything starts and ends with your heart'*. This truism is important and whilst I advocate everyone living through their heart space it is also equally important that you set strong boundaries around your heart to protect yourself.

It is also important to realise and acknowledge that there is a significant difference between a boundary and a wall. In your journey I invite you to set up boundaries as they can be moved and are not fixed, whereas a wall is permanent and needs to be knocked down or blasted away. Walls will keep you stuck, slow you on your journey, and will impede your heart connection.

The boundaries that you set need to be porous so that your heart, once connected, can shine, come forth and be heard. You will instinctively know what boundaries you need to set as they will be aligned with you and your core values and these will become evident as you undertake your Heart Whispers, Heart Trysts and all the hearting exercises and heart activation exercises in this Book.

It is also important on your hearting journey to realise that whilst everything starts and ends with your heart, it is imperative that you integrate your multiple brains into your decision-making process, and this is where I would like to introduce you to the fascinating word of *m*Braining.

*m*BRAINING – RECONNECTING WITH YOUR MULTIPLE BRAINS

*m*Braining is where neuroscience validates ancient wisdom and mysticism and it surprisingly shows us that we all have multiple brains, the head brain (Cephalic); the heart brain (Cardiac) and the gut brain (Enteric).

I invite you to reconnect with your multiple brains and come from your heart and be the best version of you in all ways. A soul who has authentic connection and compassion for yourself and the world around you. Remember, you are not a human 'being', you are a human 'becoming'.

WHAT CONSTITUTES A BRAIN?

In relation to what constitutes a brain the basic scientific and neurological position posits that your brain can be defined as having large numbers of neurons and ganglia, including sensory neurons and motor neurons; neural cells with inter-neurons, neurons re-entrantly interconnecting with other neurons; support cells and components such as glial cells, astrocytes, and proteins etc.

Also, your brain has functional attributes that perceive, assimilate and process information and can provide memory storage and access as well as the ability to mediate complex reflexes via your intrinsic nervous system.

Your brain can be viewed as a chemical warehouse of neurotransmitters and those found in your head brain are also found in your heart and gut brains. Your Head brain has approximately 86 billion neurons. Your Heart brain has between 40,000 and 120,000 neurons and your Gut brain has over 500 million neurons and has the equivalent size and complexity of some-thing like a cat's brain.

WHAT IS *M*BRAINING?

*m*Braining is the way in which you use your multiple brains and how you align and integrate your brains to focus on issues that are important to you. Once you identify your issues you can then take the necessary steps to make positive and empowered decisions in your life.

In *m*Braining your brains have what is termed 'highest levels of expression' as well as individual 'prime functions' and these are critical to how you deal with issues and make decisions in your life and these are represented in the table below:

mBRAIN	HIGHEST EXPRESSION	PRIME FUNCTIONS
Head	Creativity	Cognitive perception; Thinking; Making meaning
Heart	Compassion	Emoting; Values; Relational Affect
Gut	Courage	Core Identity; Self-preservation; Mobilisation

When you take the time to understand and actually listen to your brains you will better recognise when they are out of align-ment. The overwhelming majority of people today make deci-sions from their head and gut and that is one of the main reasons why I am on a mission to have people connect with their hearts.

"Follow your heart but take your brain with you"
ALFRED ADLER

"Brains are awesome. I wish every-body had one"
UNKNOWN

You know that feeling when you want to do something, but you can't quite take the action required? Or when your heart says one thing and your head says another? Or you have made a decision – but it doesn't 'feel right'? That is your brains not being in alignment, the feelings are surprisingly palpable.

When your *m*Brains communicate and their prime functions are in alignment then they reach their highest level of expression and it is at this point that wisdom is generated and it is through this wisdom that your decision making and life is impacted at a deep level.

*m*Braining is important for when you are – goal/outcome setting; decision making; problem solving; motivating yourself and action taking; harnessing your intuition; cultivating your own understanding and perspective on issues; dealing with your relationships; undertaking personal development, learning and behavioral changes and also focusing on your health and wellbeing. It is a powerful tool that will help transform you and your life.

I would also highly recommend that if you want to experience a deeper connection and integration that you speak with a certified *m*BIT Coach and journey with them as well. You will not regret it!

If you are drawn towards *m*Braining I encourage you to purchase and read this amazing book - Soosalu, G., and Oka, Marvin., (2012) *m*Braining: Using your Multiple Brains to do cool stuff. Time Binding Publications.

HIDDEN HEART LEARNINGS - YOUR PERSONAL VALUES

Your personal values are desirable goals that motivate your actions and serve as guideposts in your life. Everyone has values and each person has a different value set that are shaped by your personal upbringing, life experiences, culture, and many other factors.

Your values represent what is important to you and you use your values to help guide your decision making in all aspects of your life such as your own self-identity, career, religious beliefs, social circles, and friendship groups etc.

Who do you feel you truly are?

Your values influence what you do and the decisions you make. Values are the principles that give your life meaning. To live an empowered and transformed life it is important that you have a deeper understanding of what your core values are.

Your core values are the fundamental beliefs that you use to live your life. They are your guiding principles by which you view the world. When you live into your values you are connecting with your heart and making a commitment to be true to who you are.

Step 1 – Discovering your values?

1. I invite you to undertake the breath work that is contained in your self-care plan. It is important that you establish a heart connection with your breath work and when you have done this you can focus on completing your values statement.

2. Read the Life Values list and circle or highlight the values that align with who you are right now. If your values are not listed in the table then write your own.

3. When you complete your first list you may have 20-30 values so look deeply at your list, you may notice specific themes so put your main value on top.

4. I also invite you to think about your favourite movies and books and think about the characters in them. Who did you love and why?

5. Who did you dislike, and why?

6. What character traits and behaviors did these characters exhibit that really resonated with you? This will give you an idea of your own values.

92

"We should not allow our personal values to erode, even if others think we are peculiar"
JAMES L. FAUST

"When clearly defined, your values will simplify your decision-making process and will create fertile soil for you to flourish"
UNKNOWN

"Anything that changes your values changes your behavior"
GEORGE SHEEHAN

7. When you have completed your list, read through it again and choose your top three primary values.

1.

2.

3.

LIFE VALUES LIST

Accountable	Diverse	Inquisitiveness	Strength
Accurate	Dynamic	Insightfulness	Successful
Achievement	Effectiveness	Intelligence	Supportive
Adventurous	Efficiency	Intellectual	Teamwork
Altruistic	Elegant	Intuition	Thankfulness
Ambitious	Empathetic	Joyful	Thoroughness
Assertiveness	Enjoyment	Justice	Thoughtfulness
Balanced	Enthusiasm	Leadership	Timeliness
Best	Equality	Legacy	Tolerance
Belonging	Excellence	Love	Trustworthiness
Bold	Excited	Loyalty	Truth
Calm	Expert	Mastery	Understanding
Careful	Explorer	Obedience	Uniqueness
Challenged	Expressive	Openness	Unity
Cheerful	Fairness	Orderly	Usefulness
Committed	Family	Originality	**YOUR LIST**
Compassionate	Fitness	Perfection	*Integrity (example)*
Competitive	Focus	Positivity	
Consistency	Freedom	Preparedness	
Contentment	Fun	Professionalism	
Control	Generosity	Reliability	

Cooperation	Goodness	Resilience
Courageous	Grace	Resourceful
Courteous	Growth	Restraint
Creative	Happiness	Rigor
Curious	Health	Selflessness
Decisiveness	Helping	Sensitivity
Dependable	Honesty	Service
Determined	Honorable	Simplicity
Diligent	Humility	Spontaneity
Disciplined	Independence	Stability
Discreetness	Ingenuity	Strategic

Step 2 – Living into your values?

1. How do you feel when you look at your top three primary values (above)?
2. Are you living into the values you have chosen at the moment?
3. Take your top three values and then make a short list of sub values that support your primary value.
4. Be creative, be compassionate, be courageous and value your values.
5. Create a short Life Value Statement that puts it into action. See the following example:

LIFE VALUE STATEMENT (EXAMPLE)

Name	Dr John McSwiney
Core value	Compassion
Sub values	trust, integrity, truth, honesty, freedom, justice, communication, empowerment, unconditional love, joy, adventure.
Life value statement	I am passionate about helping people connect with their hearts and live into their best lives.

I invite you to gift yourself some time and feel into your Life Vision Statement. Reflect on where you have come from, where you are right now and where you truly want to be in your future.

MY LIFE VALUE STATEMENT

Name	
Core value	
Sub values	
Life value statement	

HIDDEN HEART LEARNINGS –
YOUR SHADOW VALUES

Your personal values, and how to discover them, were outlined in the previous heart learnings exercise. Understanding and feeling into your own personal values is important as it provides you with a clearer understanding of deeper aspects of who you are, and this is important to connect with your heart and live into your best life.

You may have acknowledged and experienced your values, however you may not have heard or spent any time connecting with and understanding your shadow values. Your shadow values exist within the dark side of your personality and can be considered as part of your disowned self.

Your shadow self represents the parts of you that you no longer want to acknowledge or want as part of you, and it exists in your subconscious. You cannot eliminate or get away from your shadow and trouble can arise in you and your life if you do not recognise it and integrate it into your life.

There are seven shadow values that we all possess on some level:

1. **Attention** – being unique, different or special
2. **Belonging** – being accepted by, connected and feeling part of a community
3. **Control** – being able to influence your circumstances, your territory, yourself and/or others
4. **Money** – being wealthy and/or having the power to do or have whatever you want
5. **Sexuality** – being able to express your sexual desires and/or preferences shamelessly
6. **Superiority** – being right, being better than yourself and/or others
7. **Validation** – being important, worthy and/or "good enough"

96

"Shadow work is the path of the heart warrior"
CARL JUNG

"Unless we do conscious work on it, the shadow is almost always projected; that is, it is neatly laid on someone or something else, so we do not have to take responsibility for it"
ROBERT JOHNSON

The biggest issue that you face isn't that you don't recognise and connect with your shadow values, it is the fact that you never discover what they truly are in the first place.

You have two predominate value types, shadow, and light. Your shadow values are the ones you effectively hide from the world due to either your shame or guilt, and they are usually even more powerful than your light values. Your light values on the other hand are the ones that you identify with and love to show off to the world. These seven shadow values have their 'light' value counterparts as highlighted below.

SHADOW	LIGHT
Attention	Appreciation
Belonging	Meaning
Control	Freedom
Money	Service
Sexuality	Love/Connection
Superiority	Evolution
Validation	Inspiration

If you ignore the existence and truth of your shadow values you will never be able to align your true values with your heart and your life.

DISCOVERING YOUR SHADOW VALUES

You are now on your journey of discovery and there are few exercises that I would invite you to undertake to identify, connect, and integrate your shadow into yourself.

EXERCISE 1 - SHADOW DISCOVERY – MONITOR YOUR EMOTIONAL REACTIONS

Your shadow is a shadow for a reason as it is elusive and does not want to be recognised and your Ego effectively keeps your shadow repressed and well-hidden to protect you.

As you go about your day, I invite you to pay close attention to your behavior and emotions as you will tend to project your shadow onto others in your life.

It can be difficult to journal every single behavior and emotion, but I invite you to gift yourself 10-15 minutes every day to reflect on your interactions with others and your own emotional reactions because whatever irritates and bothers you in someone else is highly likely to be a part of your own shadow.

If someone evokes an emotional reaction or charge within you, it is a beautiful breadcrumb that will lead you to your shadow, so follow it!

EXERCISE 2 - SHADOW DISCOVERY – QUESTION YOUR LIGHT

You consciously project an image to the world that you are a good person and offer up your light values as evidence and proof that this is the case. As you grew up you may have been praised for things you were good at, or you did well, and those positive affirmations became a part of your outward persona.

I invite you to make a list of all your positive qualities and their opposite. After you have done this, identify that opposite within yourself. For example, if you consider yourself to be a calm and peaceful person you may be repressing your anger part. Your anger part can be hiding in the shadow.

This shadow anger can lurk in the background and constantly challenge your peaceful part. So, identify this angry part. See it for what it truly is and accept it as a part of who you are. Make friends with it because it is ok to be angry too.

EXERCISE 3 - SHADOW DISCOVERY – YOUR 3-2-1

I invite you to spend a bit of time working with your shadow using a beautifully designed shadow integration technique developed by Mr. Ken Wilbur in his book titled, '*Integral Life Practice: A 21st-Century Blueprint for Physical Health, Emotional Balance, Mental Clarity, and Spiritual Awakening.*'

Here are the five basic steps to your 3-2-1 practice:

STEP 1: Choose a person who you have a real connection with (e.g., partner, relative, boss)

This particular person should be someone who you have a strong emotional charge with either positively or negatively.

STEP 2: Describe the qualities and characteristics of the person you have selected that may trigger you, either positively or negatively.

Talk to them out loud, or journal, in 3rd person language (he, she, it) about the positive or negative qualities or characteristics they possess and that you have felt and observed.

It is important to really feel into your heart and fully express your feelings and emotions.

STEP 3: Communicate_verbally in the 2nd person (your language) with this person in your imagination. When you are communicating with this person talk to them as if they were directly in front of you and tell them what disturbs and upsets you about them.

Ask them questions such as:

Why are you doing this to me?

What do you want from me?

What are you trying to show me?

What do you have to teach me?

After you ask the questions imagine what their responses are and speak to them out loud and record the conversation in your journal if you feel comfortable doing so.

STEP 4: Transform into this person and take on all of the qualities and characteristics that annoy, fascinate or trigger you.

Now embody all these traits and use 1st person language (I, me, mine) and describe yourself using the following type of statements:

I am ...

I am ...

I am ...

I am ...

I am ...

I am ...

I am …

I am …

I am …

I am …

I am …

This can make you feel awkward, and that is ok. The traits you are embodying and feeling into are the exact traits you have been denying in yourself.

Step 5: Experience all of these disowned shadow traits that exist within yourself and truly feel into them as a part of you.

When you feel into these disowned traits you can now acknowledge and accept them into you as a real part of who you truly are.

Now you can re-own and integrate this quality in yourself.

HIDDEN HEART LEARNINGS - GRATITUDE

I invite you to construct a gentle and loving framework around your heart as well as your emotional and spiritual wellbeing.

Your Heart Whispers will certainly help you on this journey and there is another daily practice I invite you to embrace as well – gratitude.

Every day of your life you awaken to start a new day and when you do wake up what is the first thing that you think of?

What is the first thing you feel?

Gratitude allows you to truly recognise the good in your life and when you regularly and consistently focus on this you will appreciate everything associated with it on a deeper level.

Gratitude also expands your energy field to recognise that you are not alone in your journey and it humbles you to recognise this and give thanks.

Gratitude will help you focus on how you want to use your Hidden Heart Life marbles and it will benefit your emotional, physical, social and mental wellbeing as well:

- **Emotional** – increases your life satisfaction and long-term happiness as well as making you more optimistic; reduces your jealousy and lowers your chances of being depressed.
- **Physical** – lowers your blood pressure and reduces symptoms of depression; improves your sleep and increases your ability to undertake physical activity more often.
- **Social** – strengthens all of your relationships at home and professionally and increases your social networks and standing within them.
- **Mental** – increases and improves your self-esteem and self-worth as well as boosting your happiness and positivity, together with strengthening your resilience.

"Gratitude is not only the greatest of virtues but the parent of all others"
MARCUS TULLIUS CICERO

"Piglet noticed that even though he had a very small heart, it could hold a rather large amount of gratitude"
A.A. MILNE

"Gratitude turns what we have into enough"
AESOP

"When we focus on gratitude, the tide of disappointment goes out and the tide of love rushes in"
KRISTIN ARMSTRONG

HEARTING EXERCISE - YOUR OWN GRATITUDE PRACTICE

I invite you to consider these beautiful and simple gratitude exercises as small packets of self-love that will open your heart and help expand your energy field to experience your life on a different level and frequency. I am excited for you!

- When you wake up and before you go to sleep feel into your heart and give thanks for everything and every person you have in your life. Own and claim what you love and cherish and speak it out to Source.
- Take time out to truly appreciate your surroundings especially nature and give thanks for everything you can feel, see, hear, smell and taste.
- Write yourself thankyou notes all the time and read them.
- Send your partner, family and friends messages of support and love that they would not expect and tell them how you feel about them.
- Keep a gratitude journal (hard copy or your phone or iPad) and reflect on all of the great things that have happened throughout your day.
- Highlight at least one positive thing that you have achieved or learnt every day.
- Meditate on the good things in your life.
- Use social media to tell your world what you are grateful for.
- Compile a gratitude list and add one (new) thing to it every day.
- Smile often and feel into your heart for everything you have.
- Say thankyou all the time and mean it.

There are many more ways that you will show and express your gratitude and I invite you to do what feels right for you. All I suggest is that you be realistic, be adventurous and always try something new and actually focus on a person rather than things or experiences.

HIDDEN HEART LEARNINGS - YOUR HEART EXISTENCE MIRROR

I invite you to take a moment and go to section VI in the Book and look at the Hidden Heart marble year that corresponds with your current age and really feel into the timeline of your life.

Where is your heart in your life right now?

Your Heart Existence Mirror is a beautiful heart expansion and connection tool that is similar in its scope to the Wheel of Life. Your Heart Existence Mirror is a real time reflection of where you and your heart are truly situated in key areas of your life.

Your Heart Existence Mirror provides you with a 'big picture' visual representation of eight major areas of your life and where you feel your heart is in relation to each of them.

The eight Heart Existence Mirror areas are – Health and Wellbeing; Work and Career; Physical Environment; Fun and Recreation; Personal Growth; Relationships and Romance; Financial Security and Family and Friends.

You are invited to gift yourself the time and undertake a self-assessment in each Heart Existence area so that you can become more heartful of what is happening in your world to see how balanced your life truly is.

The Heart Existence Mirror will also help guide you in key areas of your life and will provide you with opportunities to use your Hidden Heart marbles in ways you may not have imagined.

HEART EXISTENCE MIRROR – TRIAL EXERCISE

I invite you to undertake a trial exercise for your Heart Existence Mirror and have a little bit of fun with it as well. You will see below that there is a table with eight sections contained within it that represent eight major areas of your life.

In each of these sections there is an image of a heart with lines drawn through it. Now get yourself a pen or a pencil (coloured

---

104

"In the centre of the cyclone, one is off the wheel of karma, of life, rising to join the Creators of the Universe, the creators of us. Here we find that we have created Them who are us"
JOHN C. LILLY

♥ **Author's Heartnote:** The Wheel of Life is a beautiful coaching tool however it is predominately completed by people from a head and Ego based perspective of their life. Your Heart Existence Mirror provides you with a framework to look at your life through a different lens and depth – your heart. It opens new and exciting possibilities for you to live into and explore on your life's journey.

♥ **Author's Heartnote:** I would like to point out that your Heart Existence Mirror is very different from your Hidden Heart Diamond. Your mirror is very much concerned with your daily life and existence on the 3D level of consciousness plain and your Hidden Heart Diamond is focused on the metaphysical realms.

pencils if you desire) and look at each of the eight sections and give it a rating out of eleven and then shade the heart in to the rating you assigned it.

I invite you to look at each section and think about it for no more than a few seconds and move to the next section until all are completed. It doesn't matter that you are not aware of what the elements are that comprise each section, all I invite you to do is look at the heading i.e., 'Work and Career' and just give it the rating you think it is. There is no right, or wrong answer here, just be honest with yourself. *When you gift yourself an eleven it is because you are 100% happy and satisfied with that area of your life. When you give yourself a zero it is because you are not happy and you have very little satisfaction in that area of your life.*)

"One day, when my face and my name are forgotten – for the wheel of life involves everyone thrown into this world in its revolving circle and mixes them finally with the dust – then I would perhaps become transparent as a breeze. And if one looks for the heroes of our times and of the past, all then just heaps of insignificant dust, they would be found blowing by the force of my currents, in my stories"
MUKTA SINGH-ZOCCHI

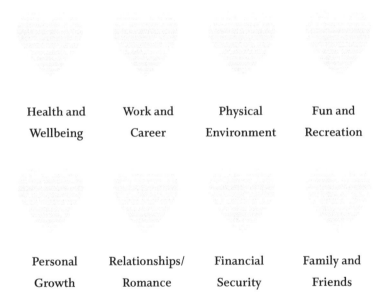

Health and Wellbeing	Work and Career	Physical Environment	Fun and Recreation
Personal Growth	Relationships/ Romance	Financial Security	Family and Friends

The trial exercise is a basic 'thinking' task, it does not come from your heart. When you complete your Heart Existence Mirror your responses will come from your heart, and not from Ego as this can provide a deeper and completely different perspective. The results between your trial exercise 'head based' and the real exercise 'heart based' may surprise you.

HEART EXISTENCE MIRROR – HEALTH AND WELLBEING

I invite you to find a safe space where you will not be disturbed and undertake your balanced heart breathing that is outlined in your Self-care Plan in this Book. It is important that you establish a heart connection with your breath work before you commence this exercise.

When you have brought yourself into balance and have made a heart connection, gift yourself the time to truly feel into the elements that comprise your Heart Existence Mirror for your Health and Wellbeing.

The elements that I invite you to reflect on, and feel into, are your:

- **Physical fitness** – Do you exercise? How regularly do you exercise? How physically healthy are you? Are you truly satisfied with your current level of physical fitness?
- **Nutrition** – Do you nourish your body with high quality foods? Do you keep yourself well hydrated? Are you truly satisfied with your current diet?
- **Sleep** – Do you have a regular sleep pattern? Do you get enough sleep? Do you wake up feeling refreshed and healed? Are you truly satisfied with your current sleep pattern?
- **Self-care** – How is your daily vitality? Do you practice healthy living? How much alcohol do you consume? Do you take drugs? Are you truly satisfied with how you take care of You?
- **Medical issues** – any prevailing or long-term illnesses? How often do you get sick or feel unwell with colds, viruses, and flus? Are you truly satisfied with your current health status?

Reflect on these Health and Wellbeing elements and feel into your heart and ask yourself about how you feel about each of these elements and how they are truly represented in your life.

106

"A healthy outside starts from the inside"
ROBERT URICH

"Health is a state of body. Wellness is a state of being"
J. STANFORD

"Day by day in every way I am getting better and better"
EMILE COUE

"Self-care is not self-indulgence, it is self-preservation"
AUDRE LORD

♥ **Author's Heartnote:** Remember this is not a 'head' or 'Ego' exercise, this is your heart telling you what it truly wants and desires for your Health and Wellbeing.

Now gift yourself a rating from zero to eleven for how much of your heart truly exists in this area of your life and shade or color the level on your Heart Existence Mirror.

Be gentle on yourself and do not increase the rating. Your heart knows, so feel into it and trust it. (*When you gift yourself an eleven it is because you are 100% happy and satisfied with that area of your life. When you give yourself a zero it is because you are not happy and you have very little satisfaction in that area of your life.*)

Health and Wellbeing Mirror

When you have completed your Heart Existence Mirror, I would like you to answer the following questions as they will help you form a strategy to bring your Heart Existence Mirror (read life) back into balance.

- **Why did you give your Health and Wellbeing the rating that you did?**
- **How long has your Health and Wellbeing been the rating you gave it?**
- **How would you like your Health and Wellbeing to truly be?**
- **What will happen if you do nothing with your Health and Wellbeing?**
- **If your Health and Wellbeing rating is not an 11 what actions will you take to make it 11/11?**

- **What would a Health and Wellbeing rating of 11 look and feel like to you?**

What are 3 things you will commit yourself to doing in the next week to help you achieve the heart related outcome you want for your Health and Wellbeing? Feel into your heart and see what it truly needs and desires.

1.

2.

3.

108 *"Your work is going to fill a large part of your life, and the only way to be truly satisfied is to do what you believe is great work. And the only way to do great work is to love what you do"*
STEVE JOBS

"It takes courage to grow up and become who you really are"
E. E. CUMMINGS

"If you don't wake up in the morning excited to pick up where you left your work yesterday, you haven't found your calling"
MIKE WALLACE

Commit yourself to take action in this area of your life today and be accountable.

If you need extra encouragement then invite someone onto your team and bring them on your journey.

Who is your accountability partner?
Who is your heartbeat buddy?

HEART EXISTENCE MIRROR – WORK AND CAREER

I invite you to find a safe space where you will not be disturbed and undertake your balanced heart breathing that is outlined in your Self-care Plan in this Book. It is important that you establish a heart connection with your breath work before you commence this exercise.

When you have brought yourself into balance and have made a heart connection, gift yourself the time to truly feel into the elements that comprise your Heart Existence Mirror for your

Work and Career whether you are in business yourself or are in paid employment.

The elements that I invite you to reflect on, and feel into, are your:

- **Work Hours** – How many hours do you work a week (including travel to and from work)? Do you have a proper work/life balance? Are you truly satisfied with your current level of working hours?
- **Career Direction and Purpose** – Are you in the right role for You? Are you passionate about the work you do and are responsible for? Is your heart truly invested in what you are doing? Are you truly satisfied with your current career direction and career purpose?
- **Performance** – Are you overachieving at work? Are you just going through the motions in your role? Are you excited or bored with your role and what you do? Are you truly satisfied with how you perform in your role?
- **Environment** – Is your working environment a place you would choose for You? Does your work environment stimulate you to perform at your best? Are you truly satisfied with your current working environment (lighting, office layout etc.)?
- **Colleagues** – How are your interactions and relationships with your work colleagues (on all levels)? Is your work environment toxic? Is your work environment inclusive and collaborative? Are you truly satisfied with your current role and interaction with colleagues?

♥ Author's Heartnote: - Remember this is not a 'head' or 'Ego' exercise, this is your heart telling you what it truly wants and desires for your Work and Career.

Reflect on these Work and Career elements and feel into your heart and ask yourself about how you truly feel about each of these elements and how they are represented in your life.

Now gift yourself a rating from zero to eleven for how much of your heart truly exists in this area of your life and shade or color the level on your Heart Existence Mirror.

Be gentle on yourself and do not increase the rating. Your heart knows, so feel into it and trust it. (*When you gift yourself an eleven it is because you are 100% happy and satisfied with that area of your life. When you give yourself a zero it is because you are not happy and you have very little satisfaction in that area of your life.*)

110

Work and Career Mirror

When you have completed your Heart Existence Mirror, I would like you to answer the following questions as they will help you form a strategy to bring your Heart Existence Mirror (read life) back into balance.

- **Why did you give your Work and Career the rating that you did?**
- **How long has your Work and Career been the rating you gave it?**
- **How would you like your Work and Career to truly be?**
- **What will happen if you do nothing with your Work and Career?**
- **If your Work and Career rating is not an 11 what actions will you take to make it 11/11?**
- **What would a Work and Career rating of 11 look and feel like to you?**

What are 3 things you will commit yourself to doing in the next week to help you achieve the heart related outcome you want for your Work and Career? Feel into your heart and see what it truly needs and desires.

1.

2.

3.

Commit yourself to take action in this area of your life today and be accountable.

If you need extra encouragement then invite someone onto your team and bring them on your journey.

Who is your accountability partner?

Who is your heartbeat buddy?

HEART EXISTENCE MIRROR – PHYSICAL ENVIRONMENT

I invite you to find a safe space where you will not be disturbed and undertake your balanced heart breathing that is outlined in your Self-care Plan in this Book. It is important that you establish a heart connection with your breath work before you commence this exercise.

When you have brought yourself into balance and have made a heart connection, gift yourself the time to truly feel into the elements that comprise your Heart Existence Mirror for your Physical Environment at your work and home and wherever you spend a lot of your time.

The elements that I invite you to reflect on, and feel into, are your:

- **Home** – Are you living in your dream home? Do you live in an environment that relaxes, calms, and heals you? Do you live in an environment that empowers and inspires you?

"This physical environment is your playground of expansion, and, without it, the Universe could not expand in the way that it does"
ABRAHAM HICKS

"Reactive people are often affected by their physical environment. They find external sources to blame for their behavior"
STEPHEN COVEY

"People seeking to live spiritually must be concerned with their social and physical environment"
SULAK SIVARAKSA

Are you truly satisfied with the physical environment you are currently living in?

- **Work** – Are you working in your dream job? Do you work in an environment that empowers and inspires you? Are you truly satisfied with the physical environment you are currently working in?
- **Space and Appearance** – Do you have enough space in your life or are you cramped and feel confined and constricted? Are you truly happy with the physical appearance and aesthetics of where you are? Are you truly satisfied with the space and appearance of where you live your life?
- **Transport** – How much time do you spend in your vehicle or public transport? How do you feel about your car, motorbike, scooter, bicycle? Are you truly satisfied with your mode of transport?
- **Comfort** – Is your home comfortable? Is your workplace comfortable? Are you meeting your basic needs for comfort at both home and work? Are you truly satisfied with your overall level of comfort in your Physical Environment?
- **Natural Light and Fresh Air** – Is your home filled with natural light and fresh air? Is your workplace filled with natural light and fresh air? Do you feel you get enough natural light and fresh air? Are you truly satisfied with the amount of natural light and fresh air you receive every day in your life?

Reflect on these Physical Environment elements and feel into your heart and ask yourself about how you truly feel about each of these elements and how they are represented in your life.

Now gift yourself a rating from zero to eleven for how much of your heart truly exists in this area of your life and shade or color the level on your Heart Existence Mirror.

Be gentle on yourself and do not increase the rating. Your heart knows, so feel into it and trust it. (*When you gift yourself*

♥ **Author's Heartnote:** Remember this is not a 'head' or 'Ego' exercise, this is your heart telling you what it truly wants and desires in your Physical Environment.

an eleven it is because you are 100% happy and satisfied with that area of your life. When you give yourself a zero it's because you are not happy and you have very little satisfaction in that area of your life.)

Physical Environment Mirror

When you have completed your Heart Existence Mirror, I would like you to answer the following questions as they will help you form a strategy to bring your Heart Existence Mirror (read life) back into balance.

- **Why did you give your Physical Environment the rating that you did?**
- **How long has your Physical Environment been the rating you gave it?**
- **How would you like your Physical Environment to truly be?**
- **What will happen if you do nothing with your Physical Environment?**
- **If your Physical Environment rating is not an 11 what actions will you take to make it 11/11?**
- **What would a Physical Environment rating of 11 look and feel like to you?**

What are 3 things you will commit yourself to doing in the next week to help you achieve the heart related outcome you want for your Physical Environment? Feel into your heart and see what it truly needs and desires.

1.

2.

3.

"You don't stop having fun because you get old, you get old because you stop having fun"
UNKNOWN

"People who cannot find time for recreation are obliged sooner or later to find time for illness"
JOHN WANAMAKER

"When you stop doing things for fun you might as well be dead"
ERNEST HEMMINGWAY

Commit yourself to take action in this area of your life today and be accountable.

If you need extra encouragement then invite someone onto your team and bring them on your journey.

Who is your accountability partner?
Who is your heartbeat buddy?

HEART EXISTENCE MIRROR – FUN AND RECREATION

I invite you to find a safe space where you will not be disturbed and undertake your balanced heart breathing that is outlined in your Self-care Plan in this Book. It is important that you establish a heart connection with your breath work before you commence this exercise.

When you have brought yourself into balance and have made a heart connection, gift yourself the time to truly feel into the elements that comprise your Heart Existence Mirror for your Fun and Recreation at your work and home and wherever you spend a lot of your time.

The elements that I invite you to reflect on, and feel into, are your:

- **Leisure** – How much time do you gift yourself for your leisure pursuits? How often do you undertake your favorite leisure activities? Are you truly satisfied with the amount and quality of leisure time you are currently experiencing?

- **Hobbies** – How much time do you gift yourself for your personal hobbies? How often do you undertake your hobbies? Do you even have any hobbies? Are you truly satisfied with your ability to pursue your hobbies?

- **Passions** – Do you have any real passions in your life? How much time do you gift yourself to pursue your passions? How often do you undertake your passion activities? Are you truly satisfied with your ability to pursue your passions?

- **Laughter** – Do you laugh often? Do you smile on a regular basis? Are you truly satisfied with the level of laughter and humor in your life?

- **Adventure** – Are you an adventurous person? How often do you gift yourself the opportunity to undertake adventurous activities? Are you truly satisfied with the level of adventure in your life?

- **Joy** – Do you experience joy? How often do you experience joy in your life? Are you truly satisfied with the amount of joy you experience in your life?

♥ **Author's Heartnote:** Remember this is not a 'head' or 'Ego' exercise, this is your heart telling you what it truly wants and desires for Fun and Recreation.

Reflect on these Fun and Recreation elements and feel into your heart and ask yourself about how you truly feel about each of these elements and how they are represented in your life.

Now gift yourself a rating from zero to eleven for how much of your heart truly exists in this area of your life and shade or color the level on your Heart Existence Mirror.

Be gentle on yourself and do not increase the rating. Your heart knows, so feel into it and trust it. (*When you gift yourself an eleven it is because you are 100% happy and satisfied with that area of your life. When you give yourself a zero it is because you are not happy and you have very little satisfaction in that area of your life.*)

Fun and Recreation Mirror

When you have completed your Heart Existence Mirror, I would like you to answer the following questions as they will help you form a strategy to bring your Heart Existence Mirror (read life) back into balance.

- **Why did you give your Fun and Recreation the rating that you did?**
- **How long has your Fun and Recreation been the rating you gave it?**
- **How would you like your Fun and Recreation to truly be?**
- **What will happen if you do nothing with your Fun and Recreation?**
- **If your Fun and Recreation rating is not an 11 what actions will you take to make it 11/11?**
- **What would a Fun and Recreation rating of 11 look and feel like to you?**

What are 3 things you will commit yourself to doing in the next week to help you achieve the heart related outcome you want for your Fun and Recreation? Feel into your heart and see what it truly needs and desires.

1.

2.

3.

Commit yourself to take action in this area of your life today and be accountable.

If you need extra encouragement then invite someone onto your team and bring them on your journey.

Who is your accountability partner?
Who is your heartbeat buddy?

HEART EXISTENCE MIRROR –
PERSONAL GROWTH

I invite you to find a safe space where you will not be disturbed and undertake your balanced heart breathing that is outlined in your Self-care Plan in this Book. It is important that you establish a heart connection with your breath work before you commence this exercise.

When you have brought yourself into balance and have made a heart connection, gift yourself the time to truly feel into the elements that comprise your Heart Existence Mirror for your Personal Growth at your work and home and wherever you spend a lot of your time.

The elements that I invite you to reflect on, and feel into, are your:

- **Education and Learning** – How much time do you gift yourself for your education and learning? How often do you undertake courses, programs, seminars? How often do

"Growth is often uncomfortable, messy, and full of feelings you were not expecting. But it is necessary"
UNKNOWN

"Change is inevitable but personal growth is a choice"
BOB PROCTOR

"Personal growth is misleading because it sounds like it's going to be fun. But if we called it 'deliberately making yourself so uncomfortable it will feel like you are dying', nobody would do it"
EMILY MCDONELL

you read material related to your personal development? Are you truly satisfied with your level of education and learning?

- **Awareness** – Are you aware of your strengths and weaknesses? Are you aware of who you truly are? Are you truly aware of what is transpiring in your life? Are you truly satisfied with your current level of awareness?
- **Spirituality** – Do you have a connection with spirit (God, Energy, Universe, the Divine)? How much time do you gift yourself to connect with spirit? Do you believe you are a spiritual person? Are you truly satisfied with your spiritual self and your spiritual journey?
- **Mindfulness** – How often do you meditate? How stressful is your life? How often do you go outside? Do you focus on one task at a time? Do you allow yourself to feel all your feelings and emotions? Are you truly satisfied with your level of mindfulness in your life?

Reflect on these Personal Growth elements and feel into your heart and ask yourself about how you truly feel about each of these elements and how they are represented in your life.

Now gift yourself a rating from zero to eleven for how much of your heart truly exists in this area of your life and shade or color the level on your Heart Existence Mirror.

Be gentle on yourself and do not increase the rating. Your heart knows, so feel into it and trust it. (*When you gift yourself an eleven it is because you are 100% happy and satisfied with that area of your life. When you give yourself a zero it is because you are not happy and you have very little satisfaction in that area of your life.*)

♥ **Author's Heartnote:** Remember this is not a 'head' or 'Ego' exercise, this is your heart telling you what it truly wants and desires for Personal Growth.

Personal Growth Mirror

When you have completed your Heart Existence Mirror, I would like you to answer the following questions as they will help you form a strategy to bring your Heart Existence Mirror (read life) back into balance.

- **Why did you give your Personal Growth the rating that you did?**
- **How long has your Personal Growth been the rating you gave it?**
- **How would you like your Personal Growth to truly be?**
- **What will happen if you do nothing with your Personal Growth?**
- **If your Personal Growth rating is not an 11 what actions will you take to make it 11/11?**
- **What would a Personal Growth rating of 11 look and feel like to you?**

What are 3 things you will commit yourself to doing in the next week to help you achieve the heart related outcome you want for your Personal Growth? Feel into your heart and see what it truly needs and desires.

1.

2.

3.

Commit yourself to take action in this area of your life today and be accountable.

If you need extra encouragement then invite someone onto your team and bring them on your journey.

Who is your accountability partner?
Who is your heartbeat buddy?

HEART EXISTENCE MIRROR – RELATIONSHIPS AND ROMANCE

I invite you to find a safe space where you will not be disturbed and undertake your balanced heart breathing that is outlined in your Self-care Plan in this Book. It is important that you establish a heart connection with your breath work before you commence this exercise.

When you have brought yourself into balance and have made a heart connection, gift yourself the time to truly feel into the elements that comprise your Heart Existence Mirror for your Relationships and Romance at your work and home and wherever you spend a lot of your time.

The elements that I invite you to reflect on, and feel into, are your:

- **Partner** – How much quality time do you currently spend with your partner? Are your love languages being met by your partner? How aware are you of your partners love languages? Do you feel supported and loved by your

"There is only one happiness in this life, to love and be loved"
GEORGE SAND

"The only thing we never get enough of is love; and the only thing we never give enough of is love"
HENRY MILLAR

"If you want a relationship that looks and feels like the most amazing thing on earth, you need to treat it like it is the most amazing thing on earth"
UNKNOWN

partner? Are you truly satisfied with your relationship with your partner?

- **Communication** – How often do you communicate with your friends and loved ones? What is the quality and frequency of your communications with your friends and loved ones? Do you express your true feelings and emotions with friends and loved ones? Are you truly satisfied with your current level of communication with your friends and loved ones?

- **Intimacy, Love and Romance** – Are you a loving and romantic person? Are you an affectionate person? Are you in love with your partner? Do you love your partner? Are your sexual needs and desires being met by your partner? Is there enough romance in your life? Are you truly satisfied with your current level of intimacy, love, and romance with your partner?

- **Self** – Do you love yourself? How often do you engage in negative or destructive self-talk? Do you treat yourself with love and compassion? Are you truly satisfied with how you love and treat yourself?

♥ **Author's Heartnote:** Remember this is not a 'head' or 'Ego' exercise, this is your heart telling you what it truly wants and desires for Relationships and Romance.

121

Reflect on these Relationships and Romance elements and feel into your heart and ask yourself about how you truly feel about each of these elements and how they are represented in your life.

Now gift yourself a rating from zero to eleven for how much of your heart truly exists in this area of your life and shade or color the level on your Heart Existence Mirror.

Be gentle on yourself and do not increase the rating. Your heart knows, so feel into it and trust it. (*When you gift yourself an eleven it is because you are 100% happy and satisfied with that area of your life. When you give yourself a zero it is because you are not happy and you have very little satisfaction in that area of your life.*)

Relationships and Romance Mirror

When you have completed your Heart Existence Mirror, I would like you to answer the following questions as they will help you form a strategy to bring your Heart Existence Mirror (read life) back into balance.

- **Why did you give your Relationships and Romance the rating that you did?**
- **How long has your Relationships and Romance been the rating you gave it?**
- **How would you like your Relationships and Romance to truly be?**
- **What will happen if you do nothing with your Relationships and Romance?**
- **If your Relationships and Romance rating is not an 11 what actions will you take to make it 11/11?**
- **What would a Relationships and Romance rating of 11 look and feel like to you?**

What are 3 things you will commit yourself to doing in the next week to help you achieve the heart related outcome you want for your Relationships and Romance? Feel into your heart and see what it truly needs and desires.

1.

2.

3.

Commit yourself to take action in this area of your life today and be accountable.

If you need extra encouragement then invite someone onto your team and bring them on your journey.

Who is your accountability partner?
Who is your heartbeat buddy?

HEART EXISTENCE MIRROR –
FINANCIAL SECURITY

I invite you to find a safe space where you will not be disturbed and undertake your balanced heart breathing that is outlined in your Self-care Plan in this Book. It is important that you establish a heart connection with your breath work before you commence this exercise.

When you have brought yourself into balance and have made a heart connection, gift yourself the time to truly feel into the elements that comprise your Heart Existence Mirror for your Financial Security at your work and home and wherever you spend a lot of your time.

The elements that I invite you to reflect on, and feel into, are your:
- **Income** – What is your current income level? Is your current income level sufficient to cover all your living and life expenses? Do you possess any passive income streams?

"Financial freedom is available to those who learn about it and work for it"
ROBERT KIYOSAKI

"Every financial decision should be driven by what you value"
DAVID BECH

"When you understand that your self-worth is not determined by your net-worth, then you will have financial freedom"
SUZE ORMAN

Do you feel secure with your current income level? Are you truly satisfied with your current level of income?

- **Savings** – Do you possess any savings? Do you feel secure with your current level of savings? Are you truly satisfied with your current level of savings?
- **Investments** – Do you possess any investments? Are your investments diversified? Do you feel secure with your current level of investments? Are you truly satisfied with your current level of investments?
- **Lifestyle** – Are you living your dream life financially? Is your lifestyle truly reflective of your current financial state? Are you truly satisfied with your financial lifestyle?
- **Budgeting** – Do you have a budget? Do you live to a budget? Do you have any financial plans? Are you satisfied with your own financial management?
- **Financial Stability** – Do you own your own home? Do you own your own motor vehicle(s)? Do you own holiday house(s)? Do you have a mortgage(s)? Are you in debt? What level of financial debt are you in? Are you satisfied that you are truly financially stable?

Reflect on these Financial Security elements and feel into your heart and ask yourself about how you truly feel about each of these elements and how they are represented in your life.

Now gift yourself a rating from zero to eleven for how much of your heart truly exists in this area of your life and shade or color the level on your Heart Existence Mirror.

Be gentle on yourself and do not increase the rating. Your heart knows, so feel into it and trust it. (*When you gift yourself an eleven it is because you are 100% happy and satisfied with that area of your life. When you give yourself a zero it is because you are not happy and you have very little satisfaction in that area of your life.*)

♥ **Author's Heartnote:** Remember this is not a 'head' or 'Ego' exercise, this is your heart telling you what it truly wants and desires for Financial Security.

Financial Security Mirror

When you have completed your Heart Existence Mirror, I would like you to answer the following questions as they will help you form a strategy to bring your Heart Existence Mirror (read life) back into balance.

- **Why did you give your Financial Security the rating that you did?**
- **How long has your Financial Security been the rating you gave it?**
- **How would you like your Financial Security to truly be?**
- **What will happen if you do nothing with your Financial Security?**
- **If your Financial Security rating is not an 11 what actions will you take to make it 11/11?**
- **What would a Financial Security rating of 11 look and feel like to you?**

What are 3 things you will commit yourself to doing in the next week to help you achieve the heart related outcome you want for your Financial Security? Feel into your heart and see what it truly needs and desires.

1.

2.

3.

Commit yourself to take action in this area of your life today and be accountable.

If you need extra encouragement then invite someone onto your team and bring them on your journey.

Who is your accountability partner?
Who is your heartbeat buddy?

HEART EXISTENCE MIRROR – FAMILY AND FRIENDS

I invite you to find a safe space where you will not be disturbed and undertake your balanced heart breathing that is outlined in your Self-care Plan in this Book. It is important that you establish a heart connection with your breath work before you commence this exercise.

When you have brought yourself into balance and have made a heart connection, gift yourself the time to truly feel into the elements that comprise your Heart Existence Mirror for your Family and Friends at your work and home and wherever you spend a lot of your time.

The elements that I invite you to reflect on, and feel into, are your:

- **Family** – What is your current family situation? Do you have a loving partner? Do you have brothers and sisters? Do you have children? Do you have extended family? What are your family relationships truly like? Do you spend quality time with your family? Are you truly satisfied with your family dynamic?

126

"There are friends, there is family and then there are friends that become family"
UNKNOWN

"Anything is possible when you have the right people there to support you"
MISTY COPELAND

"You do not need a lot of money to lead a rich life. Good friends and a loving family are worth their weight in gold"
SUSAN GALE

- **Friends** – Do you have many friends? Do you spend quality time with your friends? Do you want a larger/smaller friendship group? Are you truly satisfied with your friends and your friendship group?
- **Community** – Are you an outgoing person? Are you involved in your local community? Do you belong to any community group or organisations (sporting/social)? Would you like to be more involved with your local community? Are you truly satisfied with your current level of interaction with your community?

❤ **Author's Heartnote:** Remember   *127* this is not a 'head' or 'Ego' exercise, this is your heart telling you what it truly wants and desires for Family and Friends.

Reflect on these Family and Friends elements and feel into your heart and ask yourself about how you truly feel about each of these elements and how they are represented in your life.

Now gift yourself a rating from zero to eleven for how much of your heart truly exists in this area of your life and shade or color the level on your Heart Existence Mirror.

Be gentle on yourself and do not increase the rating. Your heart knows, so feel into it and trust it. (*When you gift yourself an eleven it is because you are 100% happy and satisfied with that area of your life. When you give yourself a zero it is because you are not happy and you have very little satisfaction in that area of your life.*)

Family and Friends Mirror

When you have completed your Heart Existence Mirror, I would like you to answer the following questions as they will help you form a strategy to bring your Heart Existence Mirror (read life) back into balance.

- **Why did you give your Family and Friends the rating that you did?**
- **How long has your Family and Friends been the rating you gave it?**
- **How would you like your Family and Friends to truly be?**
- **What will happen if you do nothing with your Family and Friends?**
- **If your Family and Friends rating is not an 11 what actions will you take to make it 11/11?**
- **What would a Family and Friends rating of 11 look and feel like to you?**

What are 3 things you will commit yourself to doing in the next week to help you achieve the heart related outcome you want for your Family and Friends? Feel into your heart and see what it truly needs and desires.

1.

2.

3.

Commit yourself to take action in this area of your life today and be accountable.

If you need extra encouragement then invite someone onto your team and bring them on your journey.

Who is your accountability partner?

Who is your heartbeat buddy?

HIDDEN HEART LEARNINGS - YOUR FUTURE HEART MAP

Your life is precious, and it is important on your journey to gift yourself the opportunity to spend quality time on yourself. You may not know everything that is going to happen to you on your journey, however you can gift yourself with an outline of the type of life you truly want to live into, and that is a very special gift indeed.

Your Future Heart Map is a Life Vision statement; however, it is not written from head and Ego, it is written from your heart. It will provide you with a heartfelt focus and clarity in key areas of your life and is based on your Heart Experience Mirror.

Your Future Heart Map will provide you with a vision to align with in order to connect with your true purpose and your Hidden Heart.

What is your vision of a full and beautiful heart based life?

What does that heart based life truly look and feel like?

MY FUTURE HEART MAP

I invite you to find a safe space where you will not be disturbed and undertake your balanced heart breathing that is outlined in your Self-care Plan in this Book. It is important that you establish a heart connection with your breath work before you commence this exercise.

When you create your map, you can use it as a foundation to help empower and transform your life. Your map can be reviewed and updated regularly. I invite you to reflect on it at least annually to help guide you on your hearts journey.

I invite you to use your insights and learnings from your completed Heart Existence Mirror to help gently guide you in the creation of your Future Heart Map and consider the following questions:

- **What if you had no obstacles in your way?**

- **If you could only make one important change, what would that be?**
- **What is your key theme for your Future Heart Map?**
- **How will you celebrate your successes when you achieve your Heart Map goals?**

I invite you to gift yourself at least 60 minutes to feel into each of the eight areas and make notes in your Hidden Heart journal. The eight Future Heart Map areas are outlined below with questions to help guide you on your journey.

HEALTH AND WELLBEING

- **Physical fitness** – How often do you exercise? How regularly do you exercise? How physically healthy are you? What are your physical fitness goals?
- **Nutrition** – How do you nourish your body with high quality foods? How hydrated do you keep yourself? What is your diet and nutrition?
- **Sleep** – How regular is your sleep pattern? How much sleep do you have? How do you feel when you wake in the morning? How important is sleep to you now?
- **Self-care** – How is your daily vitality? What are your healthy living practices? How much alcohol do you consume? What medications and drugs are you taking? What are your self-care goals?
- **Medical issues** – What, if any, are your illnesses? How fit and healthy are you? What is your current health status?

WORK AND CAREER

- **Work Hours** – How many hours do you work a week (including travel to and from work)? What does your work/life balance look and feel like?
- **Career Direction and Purpose** – How are you feeling about your work role? How passionate are you about the

130

♥ **Author's Heartnote:** Your Future Heart Map is a beautiful hearting tool that I would encourage you to do every year as it is a future vision statement of your life as felt and envisaged by your heart. It is a map of what your heart truly wants, feels, and connects with to manifest in the next 12 months.

work you do and are responsible for? How is your heart truly invested in what you are doing? What does your career direction and career purpose look and feel like?

- **Performance** – How are you performing at work? How are you genuinely feeling about the work you are responsible for? What does your career performance look and feel like?
- **Environment** – How is your working environment? How does your work environment stimulate you to perform at your best? What does your working environment (lighting, office layout etc.) look and feel like?
- **Colleagues** – How are your interactions and relationships with your work colleagues (on all levels)? How positive, inclusive, collaborative, and professional is your work environment? What is your current role and interaction with your colleagues?

PHYSICAL ENVIRONMENT

- **Home** – What does your dream home look and feel like? How does your living environment relax, calm, and heal you? How does your environment you live in, empower, and inspire you? What is the physical environment you live in?
- **Work** – How is your workplace? How does your work environment empower and inspire you? What is the physical environment you work in?
- **Space and Appearance** – How much space do you have at home and work? What are the physical appearance and aesthetics of where you live and work?
- **Transport** – How much time do you spend in your vehicle or public transport? How do you feel about your car or motorbike? What does your mode of transport feel like to you?
- **Comfort** – How comfortable is your home? How comfortable is your workplace? How are your basic needs for

comfort at both home and work being met? What is your overall level of comfort in your Physical Environment?

- **Natural Light and Fresh Air** – How is your home filled with natural light and fresh air? How is your workplace filled with natural light and fresh air? What amount of natural light and fresh air do you receive every day in your life to live and thrive?

FUN AND RECREATION

- **Leisure** – How much time do you gift yourself for your leisure pursuits? How often do you undertake your favorite leisure activities? What is the amount and quality of leisure time you are experiencing?
- **Hobbies** – How much time do you gift yourself for your personal hobbies? How often do you undertake your hobbies? What are you doing to pursue your hobbies?
- **Passions** – How are your real passions in your life? How much time do you gift yourself to pursue your passions? How often do you undertake your passion activities? What are you doing to pursue your passions?
- **Laughter** – How often do you laugh? How often do you smile? What are your levels of laughter and humor in your life?
- **Adventure** – How adventurous are you? How often do you gift yourself the opportunity to undertake adventurous activities? What is the level of adventure in your life?
- **Joy** –How often do you experience joy in your life? What does joy look like in your life? What is the amount of joy you experience in your life?

PERSONAL GROWTH

- **Education and Learning** – How much time do you gift yourself for your education and learning? What courses, programs and seminars are you undertaking and have completed? How often do you read material related to your personal development? What are your education and learning goals?

- **Awareness** – What are your strengths and weaknesses? Who are you? How are you aware of what is transpiring in your life? What is your level of awareness of what is happening in your life?
- **Spirituality** – What is your connection with spirit (God, Energy, Universe, the Divine)? How much time do you gift yourself to connect with spirit? How is your spiritual journey unfolding? What is happening with your spiritual self and your spiritual journey?
- **Mindfulness** – How often do you meditate? How stressful is your life? How often do you go outside? What are you doing to focus on one task at a time? What are you doing to allow yourself to feel all your feelings and emotions? What is your level of mindfulness in your life?

RELATIONSHIPS AND ROMANCE

- **Partner** – How much quality time do you spend with your partner? How are your love languages being met by your partner? How invested are you in your partners love languages? How loved and supported do you feel by your partner? What does your relationship with your partner look and feel like?
- **Communication** – How often do you communicate with your friends and loved ones? What is the quality and frequency of your communications with your friends and loved ones? How do you express your true feelings and emotions with your friends and loved ones? What does your current level of communication with your friends and loved ones look and feel like?
- **Intimacy, Love and Romance** – How is your love life? How is your romantic life? How are you giving and receiving

love and affection? Why do you love your partner? Why are you in love with your partner? How are your sexual needs and desires being met by your partner? What is the level of intimacy, love, and romance with your partner?

- **Self** – How are you loving yourself? How often are you engaging in negative and/or destructive self-talk? How do you treat yourself with love and compassion? What are you doing to love yourself?

FINANCIAL SECURITY

- **Income** – What is your income level? How is your income level covering all your living and life expenses? What are your passive income streams? Why do you feel secure with your current income level?
- **Savings** – How are your savings? How secure are you with your level of savings? What are your savings goals?
- **Investments** – How are your investments? How are your investments diversified? How secure do you feel about your level of investments?
- **Lifestyle** – How are you feeling about your dream lifestyle? What does your dream lifestyle look and feel like?
- **Budgeting** – How is your budget? What are you budgeting for? How are your financial plans? What are your budget and financial management plans?
- **Financial Stability** – How is your financial stability in relation to your big-ticket items such as your house, motor vehicle(s), holiday home? What level of financial debt are you in (if any)? What are you doing to become financially stable?

FAMILY AND FRIENDS

- **Family** – How is your family situation? How is your relationship with your partner? How is your relationship with your brothers and sisters? How is your relationship with your parents? How is your relationship with your children? How is your relationship with your extended family? What are your family relationships like? How do you spend quality time with your family? What does your family dynamic look and feel like?

- **Friends** – How is your relationship with your friends? How much quality time are do you spend with your friends? How are you developing your friendship group? What does your friends and your friendship group look and feel like?
- **Community** – How outgoing are you in your community? How involved are you in your community? What community group(s) or organisations (sporting/social) do you belong to? What are you doing, if anything, to be more involved with your local community? What is your level of interaction with your community?

HIDDEN HEART LEARNINGS – SMART GOALS AND HEARTS GOALS

When you gift yourself the time to complete your Heart Existence Mirror and your Future Heart Map you will have a heartfelt framework for the key areas of your life.

This framework becomes your heart blueprint and I invite you to find your courage to pursue the path that your heart is guiding you to take. To assist you on this journey it is important to also set specific goals, especially those related to what your heart truly wants and desires.

In your goal setting journey, I would like to introduce you to two special and effective goal setting tools. These tools are SMART goals and HEARTS goals.

A lot of people, especially those in business use SMART goals. SMART is an acronym for **S**pecific, **M**easurable, **A**chievable, **R**ealistic and **T**imely. They are effective for what they are created to do and are good for people who like to tick boxes and

"It's your turn. It's your time. Love yourself enough to make the change you crave"
RACHEL LISKA

"If my mind can conceive it and my heart can believe it, I know I can achieve it"
JESSE JACKSON

"If you give your heart a goal, it will repay you. It's the law of the Universe"
BEAR GRYLLS

"Set your goals, follow your dreams, listen to your heart, and don't let anything stand in your way"
BRANDY JOHNSON

135

measure results. They are very head based and are useful to help you keep focus.

The one that I love (and have created for you) are HEARTS goals and I have developed these goals to assist you on your journey to find your Hidden Heart. HEARTS is an acronym for **Harmonious, Enlightened, Authentic, Radiant, Transformative** and **Service.**

HEARTS empower you to connect with your heartspace and feel into a deeper knowing of what your heart truly wants and desires. HEARTS are big picture and come from a place of deep 'knowing', they are intuitive and more spiritual in nature and will help guide you towards your best self.

Identifying your HEARTS goals needs to be a part of your life on a regular basis. If you are not a goal setter then there is no better time to start than now!

SMART goals are effective in that they enable you to split a big goal into smaller more attainable goals that can be measured. That is why I invite you to complete your HEARTS goals first as they will provide you with your 'big' hearting goal(s) and then once you have your HEARTS you can then utilise your SMART goal(s).

HEARTS GOALS

Your HEARTS goals are important to ensure that you are actually feeling into your heart and living into your best life.

Your HEARTS goals need to be felt and experienced at a deeper level. They are not just light and superficial fluff to be bypassed and ignored because they are important to you and your life journey.

As outlined earlier, HEARTS is an acronym for **Harmonious, Enlightened, Authentic, Radiant, Transformative** and **Service.**

I invite you to find a safe space where you will not be disturbed and undertake your balanced heart breathing that is outlined in your Self-care Plan in this Book. Establish a heart connection with your breath work and when you have done this you can focus on completing your HEARTS goals and let it lead you on the path you are truly meant to be taking.

Be creative, be compassionate, be courageous and use your HEARTS goals to feel into your heart and live the life you truly desire.

HARMONIOUS
- **What are you seeking to coordinate within your heart and your life?**
- **What would you like to bring back into balance within your heart?**
- **Why do you want to unite your heart in your life?**

For example, a gentle HEARTS goal might start with, 'I want to connect with my heart so I can live a more harmonious life.'

ENLIGHTENED
- **What is your heart seeking awareness of in your life?**
- **What is your heart seeking more knowledge and feelings of?**
- **Why do you wish to have an increased spiritual awareness through your heart?**

For example, building on your HEARTS goal, 'I want to connect with my heart and deal with my emotional traumas so I can live a more harmonious and lighter filled life.'

AUTHENTIC
- **Why do you need to be real with your heart?**
- **How will your heart genuinely be invested in your life journey?**
- **What are you doing with your authentic heart?**

For example, building on your HEARTS goal, 'I want to connect with my heart and deal with my emotional traumas so I can live a more harmonious and lighter filled life. I need to open my heart and truly feel into it to help me heal.'

RADIANT
- **What are you going to do to make your heart shine in your life?**
- **How are you going to connect your heart with the light?**
- **Why is it important that your heart is illuminated in your life?**

For example, building on your HEARTS goal, 'I want to connect with my heart and deal with my emotional traumas so I can live a more harmonious and lighter filled life. I want to open my heart and truly feel into it to help me heal. I am going to gift myself the time to start to truly love myself and open my heart to being vulnerable as I want to help others like me.'

TRANSFORMATIVE
- **What part of your heart and your life are you seeking to transform?**
- **Why is changing your heart and your life important?**
- **What are you willing to do to change and reshape your life through your heart?**

For example, building on your HEARTS goal, 'I want to connect with my heart and deal with my emotional traumas so I can live a more harmonious and lighter filled life. I want to open my heart and truly feel into it to help me heal. I am going to gift myself the time to start to truly love myself and open my heart to being vulnerable as I want to help others like me. Opening my heart and healing my trauma will enable me to grow in love and hold space for others who have suffered similar life journeys.'

SERVICE
- **What will your HEARTS goal mean to others?**
- **How will you choose to live your life in service to others?**
- **How will your HEARTS goal benefit the people in your life?**
- **Is there a legacy component to what you are doing?**

For example, building on your HEARTS goal, 'I want to connect with my heart and deal with my emotional traumas so I can live a more harmonious and lighter filled life. I want to open my heart and truly feel into it to help me heal. I am going to gift myself the time to start to truly love myself and open my heart to being vulnerable as I want to help others like me. Opening my heart and healing my trauma will enable me to grow in love and hold space for others who have suffered similar life journeys. With a more open and loving heart I will be able to journey more authentically in line with who I truly am, and this will empower me to assist others on their journeys with more compassion and joy.'

SMART GOALS

SMART is an acronym for Specific, Measurable, Achievable, Realistic and Timely.

The SMART Goals framework provides leading questions in each area to help guide you on your SMART goal setting journey.

I invite you to find a safe space where you will not be disturbed and undertake your balanced heart breathing that is outlined in your Self-care Plan in this Book. Establish a heart connection with your breath work and when you have done this you can focus on completing your SMART goals and let it lead you on the path you are truly meant to be taking.

Be creative, be compassionate, be courageous and use your SMART goal to feel into your heart and live the life you truly desire.

SPECIFIC
- **Who is this goal for?**
- **What do you want to accomplish with this goal?**
- **When will you achieve this goal?**
- **Where will this goal be achieved?**
- **Why do you want to achieve this goal?**

For example, a general goal would be, 'I want to connect with my heart.' A more specific goal would be, 'I want to live my best life and I am going to contact Dr John McSwiney today and make an appointment to speak with him about how I connect with my heart.'

MEASURABLE
- **How will you measure progress?**
- **What will success look like to you?**
- **What will success feel like to you?**

For example, building on the goal above, 'I want to live my best life and I am going to contact Dr John McSwiney and make an appointment to speak with him about how I connect with my heart. I am going to commit myself to complete eleven 1:1 personal sessions or enroll in one of his programs.'

ACHIEVABLE
- **Do you have the resources to obtain this goal?**
- **If not, how can you obtain them?**
- **Has anyone else successfully achieved this before?**

For example, building on the goal above, 'I want to live my best life and I am going to contact Dr John McSwiney and make an appointment to speak with him about how I connect with my heart. I am going to commit myself to complete eleven 1:1

personal sessions or enroll in one of his programs. I am committed to connecting with my heart as I know that Dr McSwiney has successfully coached many people before me.'

REALISTIC
- **Is the goal realistic for you?**
- **Are you able to commit to achieve the goal?**

For example, building on the goal above, 'I am 48 and feel like I have wasted many years of my life. I truly want to live into my best life, and I am going to contact Dr John McSwiney and make an appointment to speak with him about how I connect with my heart. I am going to commit myself to complete eleven 1:1 personal sessions or enroll in one of his programs. I am committed to connecting with my heart and will do whatever it takes to heal from my trauma, as I know that Dr McSwiney has coached many people before me.'

TIMELY
- **What is your deadline?**
- **Is your deadline realistic?**

For example, building on the goal above, 'I am 47 and feel like I have wasted many years of my life. I truly want to live into my best life, and I am going to contact Dr John McSwiney and make an appointment to speak with him about how I connect with my heart. I am going to commit myself to complete eleven 1:1 personal sessions or enroll in one of his programs. I am committed to connecting with my heart and will do whatever it takes to heal from my trauma, as I know that Dr McSwiney has coached many people before me. I will start my inwards journey with Dr John and will be a different person by my 50th birthday.'

SMART AND HEARTS GOALS PLUS – FUTURE PACE

I invite you to follow these instructions to further enhance and accomplish your SMART and HEARTS goals:

1. What is the last thing that needs to happen so you know you have achieved your goal?
2. Visualise what your goal will look like when you achieve it. How does it make you feel?
3. Are you excited?
4. Does your goal motivate you?
5. Find a safe space where you will not be disturbed and undertake your balanced heart breathing and smile, this is your future you are now creating.
6. Close your eyes and visualise yourself hovering above yourself looking down as you go through the process of making your goal a reality.
7. Who is helping you?
8. Who is keeping you accountable?
9. What resources do you need?
10. Talk to yourself about it, describe out loud what you see, feel and hear.
11. Float into the future and visualise yourself completing your goal on the date you have set yourself, see it, feel it, hear it, experience everything about it.
12. When you have floated through your goal timeline and see yourself complete it, take six deep breaths, again in through your nose and out through your mouth, open your eyes and smile.
13. Reaffirm to yourself that this goal is yours to achieve and it has been achieved.
14. Now, make your goal the reality it already is.
15. How will you celebrate your successes?

HIDDEN HEART LEARNINGS - YOUR FEELINGS AND SELF TALK

You are who you are today because of all that has happened to you in your life. Your feelings create powerful physical and behavioral responses that are more complex than just being happy or sad.

In your life there is a high likelihood that you have experienced emotional, psychological and spiritual pains, hurts and trauma. In fact you may have experienced this on multiple occasions over a prolonged period of time.

It is these events, and your subsequent responses to them that has over time disconnected you from your heart. You were doing what you needed to do to survive the experience(s) and have done nothing wrong.

In fact, you should thank yourself for being strong enough to have endured what you have, to the point that you are even reading this Book. That is a mighty achievement, and I am genuinely very happy for you.

When you experience emotional, psychological, and spiritual pains, hurts and trauma you store the memories and feelings not just inside your mind (conscious and subconscious) but also in your body as well. Over time, this storage of hurts, pain, trauma, fear, grief etc. manifests as dis-ease.

In your journey to find your hidden heart it is important that you gift yourself the opportunity to truly understand and appreciate your feelings and emotions, even the ones you have hidden away for years and even decades!

It is important that you feel into your heart and are expansive with your emotive language and label your emotions as this will in turn help to empower and transform how you feel about yourself and your life.

I invite you to find a safe space where you will not be disturbed and undertake your balanced heart breathing that is outlined in your Self-care Plan in this Book.

"Self-talk is the most powerful form of communication because it either empowers you or it defeats you"
WRIGHT THURSTON

"It's not what we say out loud that really determines our lives. It's what we whisper to ourselves that has the most power"
ROBERT KIYOSAKI

"Whether you think you can or you think you can't, you're right"
HENRY FORD

143

Establish a heart connection with your breath work and when you have done this you can focus on completing your feelings and language exercises.

Be creative, be compassionate, be courageous and complete the exercise below and look at the lists of emotive language (these are not exhaustive lists, they are reflective examples for you to use) as a reference guide to help empower your language and transform how you communicate with yourself and the world around you.

POSITIVE LANGUAGE

I invite you to read through the list of positive language and select a new positive word and use it every day. What word are you going to use right now? You even have space to write in your own.

Positive			
kind	happy	playful	calm
understanding	joy	courageous	good
confident	lucky	energetic	peaceful
reliable	fortunate	animated	freedom
easy	delighted	spirited	comfortable
amazed	overjoyed	thrilled	pleased
loved	compassionate	wonderful	unique
sympathetic	intrigued	creative	dynamic
satisfied	curious	free	tenacious
receptive	thankful	eager	contented
accepting	optimistic	keen	quiet
open	confident	hopeful	secure
affectionate	ecstatic	inspired	relaxed
sensitive	satisfied	determined	strong
tender	glad	excited	positive
devoted	cheerful	enthusiastic	bold

**HEARTING QUESTIONS FOR
POSITIVE LANGUAGE**

When you look through the list of positive words how does it make you feel?

- *What is coming up for you?*

- *When was the last time you were aware of using positive language about yourself and your life?*

- *What would your life be like if you used positive language every day?*

What are 3 things you will commit yourself to doing in the next week to help you use positive language in your life? Feel into your heart and see what it truly wants and desires.

1.

2.

3.

Commit yourself to take action in this area of your life today and be accountable.

If you need extra encouragement then invite someone onto your team and bring them on your journey.

Who is your positive language accountability partner?

NEGATIVE LANGUAGE

Negative language can have a devastating impact on you and how you live and experience your life. I invite you to read through the list of negative language, and see how many negative words you use, or feel on a regular basis. You even have space to write in your own.

Negative			
angry	depressed	confused	helpless
irritated	scared	upset	incapable
nervous	disappointed	doubtful	alone
hostile	discouraged	uncertain	paralysed
insulting	ashamed	indecisive	fatigued
injured	powerless	perplexed	useless
annoyed	rejected	embarrassed	inferior
upset	guilty	hesitant	vulnerable
hateful	dissatisfied	shy	empty
unpleasant	miserable	pathetic	forced
offensive	detestable	disillusioned	hesitant
bitter	repugnant	unbelieving	despair
aggressive	despicable	skeptical	frustrated
resentful	disgusting	distrustful	distressed
incensed	hurt	pessimistic	rejected
suspicious	sad	afraid	hurt

HEARTING QUESTIONS FOR NEGATIVE LANGUAGE

- *When you look through the list of negative words how does it make you feel?*

- *What is coming up for you?*

- *When was the last time you were aware of using negative language about yourself and your life?*

- *What would your life be like if you did not use negative language every day?*

What are 3 things you will commit yourself to doing in the next week to help you stop using negative language in your life? Feel into your heart and see what it truly wants and desires.

1.

2.

3.

Commit yourself to take action in this area of your life today and be accountable.

If you need extra encouragement then invite someone onto your team and bring them on your journey.

Who is your negative language accountability partner?

HIDDEN HEART LEARNINGS – WHAT BRINGS YOU JOY?

Your life is precious and it is important that you spend time doing what you love and using your Hidden Heart Life marbles on the things that bring you joy and empower you to be the best you can be.

Joy is a feeling of great pleasure and happiness and is so important to experience and live into on a regular basis to help grow and strengthen your heart connection. When you

"Find out where joy resides and give it a voice far beyond singing. For to miss the joy is to miss all"
ROBERT LOUIS STEVENSON

"The more the heart is sated with joy, the more it becomes insatiable"
GABRIELLE ROY

"Joy does not simply happen to us. We have to choose joy and keep choosing it every day"
HENRI NOUWEN

"Go find your joy. Whatever that is, go find your joy. Are you going to have a good day, or are you going to have a great day? Because it's completely up to you"
SANDRA BULLOCK

147

experience true joy, you feel different, and you see and interact with the world at a different level and frequency.

The state of joy has a resonance that attracts the same in others. When you are more joyous you attract more joyous people and experiences into your life. Joy also helps you to bring balance to your life in that it detaches you from your head and drops you into your heart.

I invite you to consider what I am about to say, you often feel tired, not because you have done too much, but because you have done too little of what sparks a light in you; that light is joy.

It is so important to live into a life that sparks joy. Everyone's joys are different and need to be experienced and felt at a deep heart level. However, over time external pressures and traumas can squeeze your capacity to even glimpse joy. Joy becomes a zephyr that can never be felt or even seen.

Gift yourself time and feel into your heartspace and ask it what it truly feels and truly wants to reconnect with joy. Start small and make joy a part of your daily life. Really feel it and experience it.

WHAT ARE YOUR JOYS?

I invite you to find a safe space where you will not be disturbed and undertake your balanced heart breathing that is outlined in your Self-care Plan in this Book.

Establish a heart connection with your breath work and when you have done this you can focus on feeling into what brings you joy. Start with something small and progress from there.

You may also find that you are unable to remember something that brings you joy. This is perfectly ok, think back to when you were younger, what brought you joy then?

148 *"Rarely does tiredness come from a lack of sleep. It comes from a lack of peace"*
LINCOLN INNIS

MY TOP 11 JOYS IN LIFE

1.

2.

3.

4.

5.

6.

7.

8.

9.

10.

11.

"*If you feel 'burnout' setting in, if you feel demoralized and exhausted, it is best, for the sake of everyone, to withdraw and RESTORE yourself*"

DALAI LAMA

It is important to review your list regularly and feel into your heart and be honest with yourself. Your list is important because it will provide you with an indication of how you are feeling about your life.

I invite you to complete a little exercise to unpack each of your top eleven joys so you can experience them more in your life. In your journal use the following headings to go deeper into each of your joys. The headings are joy, feelings, frequency, and blocks. Use the following example as a guide:

EXAMPLE

Joy – I love to surf.

Feelings – When I surf, I feel totally alive and full of energy.

Frequency – I would like to surf at least once a week.

Blocks – I need to gift myself time and do it.

HEARTING QUESTIONS - JOY

- *When you look through your joy list how does it make you feel?*

- *What is coming up for you?*

- *When was the last time you experienced joy in your life?*

- *What would your life be like if you experienced joy every day?*

- *Would you like more joy in your life?*

- *What is stopping you from experiencing joy?*

You have a choice to maintain your status quo or take action.

What 3 things will you do this week to experience joy and who will you have to keep you accountable?

1.

2.

3.

Commit yourself to take action in this area of your life today and be accountable.

If you need extra encouragement then invite someone onto your team and bring them on your journey.

Who is your Joy accountability partner?

PART V

EXCEPTIONAL HEARTING SELF-CARE

154

"If compassion does not include yourself, it is incomplete"
JACK KORNFIELD

"Self-care is not self-indulgence, it is self-preservation"
AUDRIE LORDE

"Rest and self-care are so important. When you take time to replenish your spirit, it allows you to serve from the overflow. You cannot serve from an empty vessel"
ELEANOR BROWN

In the Book the primary focus is on you connecting with your heart, and a very important aspect of your connection relates to self-care. Your self-care is critical for you to function at a high level with a compassionate heart and live into your best life.

I invite you to go and find your Heart Connection Oath; you know, the one that you signed and read out loud to yourself in front of a mirror. Now read your Oath again and have a look at the second last dot point. If you do not have it with you, it is on the following page.

HEART CONNECTION OATH

I, ..., place my hand on my heart and swear that:

- I will fully invest myself into undertaking an intensive, compassionate, and guided encounter with my heart
- I will commit to read *The Journey of 100 Hidden Hearts*
- I will commit to feel into my heart and undertake all Hidden Heart Whispers, Hidden Heart Trysts, and the completion of all the Hidden Hearting exercises and activation tasks contained in the Book
- I will be emotionally and spiritually available for everything I need to do
- I will be courageous, creative, compassionate, and authentic
- I will be truthful and respectful with myself and others
- I will be honest with yourself and others
- I will be fully present during my heart connection journey
- **I will establish an exceptional self-care practice**
- I will be available for your Heartbeat Buddy

Do you remember that you signed and dated this Oath promising to honour yourself to undertake exceptional self-care? So, feel into your heart, gift yourself compassion, and embrace this part of your beautiful journey.

When you commit to self-care throughout your life you are committing to valuing all aspects of yourself. Self-care is about loving and nurturing your physical, mental, spiritual and emotional wellbeing.

WHAT DOES SELF-CARE LOOK LIKE?

Self-care is you undertaking activities and practices that gift you energy, empower you, lower your stress levels and contribute to your overall physical, mental, spiritual and emotional wellbeing.

It is important for you to recognise and acknowledge that when you are feeling stressed, anxious or tense, that you have the tools and understanding to manage yourself through these moments.

I invite you to make a commitment to yourself right now that you will acknowledge that your physical, mental, spiritual, and emotional health and wellbeing are areas of your life that you will manage and safeguard now and into your future. Here are key areas you can focus on:

- Exercise and Physical Activity
- Nourishment
- Water and Hydration
- Breathing
- Sleep
- Mindfulness
- Experiencing Joy

SELF-CARE IS A DAILY AND LONG-TERM PURSUIT

Your self-care regimen will take daily practice, it is not an opt in and opt out activity. Like all things that take practice, you need to have patience and be kind to yourself in the process.

I invite you to consider an Olympic athlete, in order for them to perform at their best they undertake a holistic approach to their training. An Olympian's self-care plan also includes many of the activities that are a part of your Hidden Heart journey.

You need to practice self-care in all aspects of your life so you can perform at your best. I invite you to spend some time perusing the self-care plan in the Book and you engage it with an open heart and make it, and yourself, a priority.

SELF-CARE PLAN – PRACTICE SELF-CARE

Your self-care is critical for you to help connect with your heart, and for you to live into your best life. It covers a range of practices and activities that involve you being kind to yourself and treating yourself with integrity, compassion, and respect.

When you practice self-care you feel healthy, calm and rested. Ask yourself this question – Are you a 'human being' or a 'human doing'? To live into an empowered and transformed life one essential habit you need to develop is feeling into your heart and practicing self-care through it. Your heart knows, so listen to it.

I invite you to look at the table below and for each self-care category give yourself a rating from 0-11 with 0 being poor and 11 being ideal and feel into your heart, and be honest with your responses.

"You are not the sun. You are not responsible for everyone's life on the planet"
UNKNOWN

"Every time you make a commitment to your own self-care, self-love and self-respect and then follow through, you build trust in yourself"
MIRANDA J. BARRETT

Self-Care Category	Rating (0-11)
Exercise and Physical Activity	
Nourishment	
Water and Hydration	
Breathing	
Sleep	
Mindfulness	
Experiencing Joy	

I invite you to look at your responses and take a moment to reflect on how you have rated these areas of your life. Now feel into your heart and answer the following questions:

- **Are there any patterns in your responses?**

- What stands out for you?
- What would you like to change?
- What is one action you can take today in every category to move towards improving where you are right now?

CREATE YOUR OWN SELF-CARE LIFE PLAN

I invite you to use the interactive table to create your own professional self-care life plan that you can use to commence your exceptional self-care regime. So, take your time, practice self-love and enjoy your journey.

Step 1 - Select one or more of the Life Categories from your list on the Table.

Step 2 - For each category that you know you want to focus on write down the activities or strategies that you would like to implement that will empower and enhance your life and your wellbeing.

Step 3 - List the barriers and limiting beliefs (either real or imagined) that may hinder or even stop you accomplishing your professional self-care life goals.

Step 4 - Be honest about your current life circumstances and feel the ways to overcome and find remedies for these barriers and limiting beliefs.

Step 5 - Act today!

Make your self-care life plan visual and put it in a place where you can see it every day. Self-care is about you empowering and transforming your life experience.

♥ **Author's Heartnote:** Feel into your heart and be truly honest with your responses for they can become very powerful tools to help you identify and heal old hurts, pains, wounds, and traumas.

SELF-CARE CATEGORY – SLEEP – (EXAMPLE)

ACTIVITY	BARRIERS	REMEDY(S)
Sleep	Staying up late on social media. Drinking coffee at night. Not dealing with my anxiety and stress	Switch my phone off at 10pm. No coffee after lunch. Speak with someone to help manage with my stress and anxiety

SELF-CARE CATEGORY –

ACTIVITY	BARRIERS	REMEDY(S)

Self-care is different for every person and it is important that you take some time and really feel into what works best for you, ask your heart what it truly needs, it knows and will tell you!

Self-care is about you making a choice to put yourself first, you need to choose to do it, it will not magically happen around you. Gift yourself permission to connect with your heart and feel what it is telling you. Everything starts and ends with your heart, so trust it and start living into your best life.

SELF-CARE PLAN – EXERCISE AND PHYSICAL ACTIVITY

Would you be surprised if I was to tell you that regular physical activity is one of the best things you can do for the health and wellbeing of your heart?

Exercise and physical activity are great medicine for you and your life. I invite you to make time and include it in your daily activities! So, what exactly are exercise and physical activity?:

Exercise is a subset of physical activity that is planned, structured and repetitive and has an end goal to be physically fit.

Physical activity is defined by the World Health Organisation as any bodily movement produced by skeletal muscles that requires energy expenditure. Physical activity refers to all movement including leisure time, for transport to get to and from places, or as part of your work.

EXERCISE AND PHYSICAL ACTIVITY BENEFITS

There are many benefits of exercising and being physically active. When you gift yourself the time to exercise regularly you can:

- reduce your risk of heart attack
- manage your weight better
- lower your cholesterol levels
- lower your risk of type 2 diabetes and some cancers
- lower your blood pressure
- have stronger bones, muscles and joints and lower your risk of osteoporosis
- recover better from periods of hospitialisation or prolonged bedrest

A number of studies have also found that exercise can improve your state of mind and help with negative and depressive thoughts in that:

160

"Exercise not only changes your body, it changes your mind, your attitude, and your mood"
UNKNOWN

"Take care of your body. It's the only place you have got to live"
JIM ROHN

"The hardest thing about doing exercise is to start doing it. Once you are doing exercise regularly, the hardest thing is to stop"
ERIN GRAY

- exercise can block negative thoughts or distract you from daily worries
- exercising with others provides an opportunity for increased social contact
- increased fitness can lift your mood and improve your sleep patterns
- exercise can also change the levels of chemicals in your brain, such as serotonin, endorphins, and stress hormones

HOW TO GET STARTED

I invite you to consider taking a gentle approach in starting your exercise and physical activity journey:

- **Start small** - Begin by making time in your day to exercise, even if it is just for a short walk. You then build your routine gradually every day. Every step and every minute counts.
- **Be realistic and kind to yourself** - If you are new to exercise, or have not exercised in a long time, be kind and gentle with yourself. Create a plan to start exercising for 11 minutes a day and increase your motivation to keep going.
- **Discover your neighbourhood** - Go for a walk or a ride around your neighborhood. Connect with your local surroundings and make a plan of all the places where you will exercise next.
- **Variety is important** – Exercise is more enjoyable when you know it is fun. Gift yourself the opportunity to connect with your inner child and do something that you know they want you to do. Here are a few suggestions – walking, running, swimming, yoga, skipping cycling, martial arts, paddle boarding … your list is endless and only limited by your imagination.
- **Be accountable** – Exercise and physical activity is something you can do by yourself or with others. Find yourself a

good accountability buddy and get them involved in what you are doing and what you want to achieve.

- **Be prepared** - Make sure that when you exercise that you have the proper gear for what you are doing, carry water and avoid injuries. You may even want to use an exercise monitor like a Fitbit or a watch/device that measures your heart rate and other important information that you can use to keep motivated.
- **Be safe** – You know what you are capable of, and it is important that you keep yourself safe and do not overexert yourself. If you are exercising outside, make sure it is in a safe environment for you and if you are wearing headphones be mindful of what is around you.
- **Join a gym or community organisation** – Being part of a group can really help empower you to achieve your exercise goals and it also a great way to meet people who like the things that you do. Speak with family and friends or Google what groups and organisations you have in your area.

YOUR BASIC EXERCISE PLAN

Your exercise plan is a very simple way to help organise your week and motivate you to literally step up and become active and fully engaged with your physical wellbeing. Your plan can teach you new things and make it easier to be more accountable, proficient and build healthy habits.

EXERCISE ACTIVITIES - (EXAMPLE)

JOGGING	SWIMMING	CYCLING	(EXERCISE)	(EXERCISE)
3 x per week 5km	3 x per week 30-minute pool session	1 x per week 20km flat ride	(Frequency)	(Frequency)

162 ♥ **Author's Heartnote:** Before you get started, I would highlight a word of caution. It is a good idea that you speak with your doctor if you have any concerns about your health and before starting any exercise program. A pre-exercise screening can identify any medical conditions that may need to be managed. Gift yourself a safety net to decide if the potential benefits of exercise outweigh any potential risks for you.

EXERCISE TRACKER – (EXAMPLE)

ACTIVITY	MON	TUE	WED	THU	FRI	SAT	SUN
Jogging	yes	no	no	no	no	no	no
Swimming	yes	no	no	yes	no	no	yes
Cycling	no	no	no	no	no	yes	no

I invite you to take a moment and gift yourself the opportunity to feel into the life you want to be living. A life that includes exercise and physical activity. You are never too old, and you will find time if it is important to you. Start small and take it one step at a time.

EXERCISE ACTIVITIES

(Exercise)　　(Exercise)　　(Exercise)　　(Exercise)　　(Exercise)

(Frequency)　(Frequency)　(Frequency)　(Frequency)　(Frequency)

EXERCISE TRACKER

ACTIVITY	MON	TUE	WED	THU	FRI	SAT	SUN

HEARTING QUESTIONS – EXERCISE AND PHYSICAL ACTIVITY

- *When you look at exercise and physical activity how does it make you feel?*

- *What is coming up for you?*

- *When was the last time you focused on exercise and physical activity in your life?*

- *What would your life be like if you spent time engaged in exercise and physical activity every day?*

- *Would you like more energy, drive and stamina in your life?*

- *What is stopping you from gifting yourself time to exercise?*

- *You have a choice to maintain your status quo or take action.*

What 3 things will you do this week to gift yourself time to exercise and who will you have to keep you accountable?

1.

2.

3.

Commit yourself to take action in this area of your life today and be accountable.

If you need extra encouragement then invite someone onto your team and bring them on your journey.

Who is your exercise accountability partner?

SELF-CARE PLAN – BREATHING

Breathing techniques are a powerful means for you to reconnect with and align your heart physiologically and spiritually with your human presence or consciousness.

I invite you to consider the last time you thought about your breathing? It is not just critical for your survival it is also critical for you to reconnect and open your beautiful heart.

Your breathing releases 70% of the toxins in your body including dangerous carbon monoxide (the other 30% being released through your bowels and bladder).

Your breath is more powerful than you can imagine as it actually connects your mind and your body. Breathing at the most basic level will keep you alive, however it is also a powerful tool to help you relax and achieve a clear state of mind and help align your head, your heart and your gut (multiple brains).

I invite you to empower yourself with your breathing and learn to use it to benefit every part of your life. The first breathing exercise I have for you is very simple to learn especially if you have never attempted any breathing exercises before.

The other exercises are more advanced, and are easy to master. Remember, all of these exercises will help you to connect with your heart space, relax, relieve stress and empower you.

EXERCISE 1 – BELLY (OR STOMACH) BREATHING
Belly breathing is easy to do and very relaxing. Try this basic exercise anytime you need to relax or relieve stress.

"The greatest luxury of life is peaceful breathing because it repairs the wounds of the cosmic soul"
AMIT RAY

"Sometimes the most important thing in a whole day is the rest we take between two breaths"
UNKNOWN

"Breathing is meditation: Life is meditation. You have to breathe in order to live, so breathing is how you get in touch with the sacred space of your heart"
WILLOW SMITH

1. Sit or lie flat in a comfortable position and close your eyes.

2. Put one hand on your belly just below your ribs and the other hand on your chest.

3. Take a deep breath in through your nose, and let your belly push your hand out. Your chest should not move. (Imagine your belly is a balloon and you are blowing it up.)

4. Breathe out through closed lips as if you were whistling. Feel the hand on your belly go in, and use it to push all the air out.

5. Do this breathing three to ten times. Take your time with each breath.

6. Notice how you feel at the end of the exercise.

EXERCISE 2 - BALANCED HEART BREATHING

Balanced Heart breathing is designed to align you with your heart and to open up your higher consciousness to receive understanding, knowledge and wisdom.

When you are feeling stressed, anxious or nervous about an issue or problem and you need guidance or clarification on something, I invite you to take a moment and do your balanced heart breathing and really feel into what your heart truly needs and desires.

1. Sit or lie flat in a comfortable position and close your eyes.

2. Put one hand on your belly just below your ribs and the other hand on your chest just over your heart space.

3. Take a deep breath in through your nose for 6 seconds and let your belly push your hand out. Your chest should not move. (Imagine your belly is a balloon and you are blowing it up.)

4. Breathe out through closed lips for 6 seconds as if you were whistling. Feel the hand on your belly go in, and use it to push all the air out.

5. (*Optional but highly recommended*) – as you breathe in imagine that each breath has a color associated with it and that this color also contains energy and power that is calming and healing for you. Every breath you inhale contains this powerful colorful healing energy. Breathe it into your heart space and into your belly and feel it flow through your entire body. Feel the power and the energy release inside you with every breath. Now imagine that when you are breathing out that every breath out contains within it, the stress, the tension, the anxiety, the pain. The fear, the hurt, the torment and any other negative feeling or emotion or limiting belief that you are holding inside of you. Breathe these negative energies out and release them to the Universe.

6. Do this breathing until you feel a sense of calm and peace and then feel into your heart space and ask your heart for guidance.

7. Notice how you feel at the end of the exercise.

EXERCISE 3 – 4-7-8 BREATHING

4-7-8 breathing is a natural tranquiliser for your nervous system and I invite you to undertake this breathing exercise when you are feeling uber stressed.

1. Sit or lie flat in a comfortable position and close your eyes.

2. Put one hand on your belly and the other on your chest as in the belly breathing exercise.

3. Exhale completely through your mouth, making a whoosh sound.

4. Close your mouth and inhale quietly through your nose for 4 seconds.

5. Hold your breath and silently count from 1 to 7.

6. Exhale completely through your mouth for 8 seconds and make a woosh sound as you breathe out.

7.   This is one breath. Now inhale again and repeat the cycle three more times for a total of four breaths.

8.   Notice how you feel at the end of the exercise.

You can try these breathing exercises straight away and I invite you to take the time to experiment with different types of breathing techniques and to dedicate time through your day to reconnect and be fully present with your breathing and with your heart.

HEARTING QUESTIONS - BREATHING

- *When you look at the breathing exercises how do they make you feel?*

- *What is coming up for you?*

- *When was the last time you focused on just your breathing in your life?*

- *What would your life be like if you spent time engaged in these breathing techniques every day?*

- *Would you like more balance, peace, and clarity in your life?*

- *What is stopping you from gifting yourself time to breathe?*

You have a choice to maintain your status quo or take action.

What 3 things will you do this week to gift yourself time to breathe and who will you have to keep you accountable?

1.

2.

3.

Commit yourself to take action in this area of your life today and be accountable.

If you need extra encouragement then invite someone onto your team and bring them on your journey.

Who is your breathing accountability partner?

SELF-CARE PLAN - WATER AND HYDRATION

Proper hydration is great not just for your brain, your attitude and your general wellbeing, it is also critical for your heart to perform at its best!

Your heart is constantly working and pumping about 6000 litres/2,000 gallons of blood a day through your body. When you choose to stay hydrated, i.e. drinking more water than you are losing you are helping your heart to beat.

I invite you to consider the fact that every cell, tissue, and organ in your body needs water to function and work properly. Keeping hydrated is crucial for your health and well-being as between 50 - 80% of your body is made up of water and 90% of your blood is water.

Empowerment and transformation is possible when you are balanced in all areas of your life including your health and well-being. The *Newsletter of Medical News Today* outlined 15 key benefits of drinking water and keeping hydrated:

"We never know the worth of water until the well is dry"
FRENCH PROVERB

"Get sleep. Eat clean. Drink water. Exercise. Repeat"
UNKNOWN

"When you feel thirsty you are already dehydrated"
UNKNOWN

"Pure water is the world's first and foremost medicine"
SLOVAKIAN PROVERB

169

1.   It lubricates the joints
2.   It forms saliva and mucus
3.   It delivers oxygen throughout the body
4.   It boosts skin health and beauty
5.   It cushions the brain, spinal cord, and other sensitive tissues
6.   It regulates body temperature
7.   The digestive system depends on it
8.   It flushes body waste
9.   It helps maintain blood pressure
10. The airways need it
11. It makes minerals and nutrients accessible
12. It prevents kidney damage
13. It boosts performance during exercise
14. Weight loss
15. It reduces the chance of a hangover

I invite you to consider using this water consumption table. It will provide an outline of how well hydrated you are keeping yourself. So help yourself today and start keeping track of what and how much you drink.

It is commonly recommended that you drink around eight 220mls (8 ounce) glasses of water every day. I invite you to make this a reality in your life from this day moving forward.

MY PERSONAL WATER CONSUMPTION TABLE			
	Fluid	Quantity	Time
Monday			
Tuesday			

Wednesday

Thursday

Friday

Saturday

Sunday

Do you consume enough water each day?

How much water have you actually consumed today?

Here are some ideas for how you can be sure you drink enough:

- Carry a water bottle with you wherever you go. This way you can drink whenever you need to.
- Keep track of your intake. Aim to take in optimum amounts every day, a minimum of half your body weight in ounces.
- Pace yourself to approach half of your recommended consumption by midday. You can always finish about an hour before you plan to sleep.

"Do something today that your future self will thank you for"
ANONYMOUS

**HEARTING QUESTIONS –
WATER AND HYDRATION**

- *When you look at the effect that water and hydration has on you how does it make you feel?*

- *What is coming up for you?*

- *When was the last time you acknowledged how important water and hydration is in your life?*

- *What would your life be like if you hydrated yourself properly every day?*

- *Would you like to be at your optimum in your life?*

- *What is stopping you from hydrating yourself effectively every day?*

You have a choice to maintain your status quo or take action.

What 3 things will you do this week to gift yourself time to hydrate yourself effectively, and who will you have to keep you accountable?

1.

2.

3.

Commit yourself to take action in this area of your life today and be accountable.

If you need extra encouragement then invite someone onto your team and bring them on your journey.

Who is your hydration accountability partner?

172

"Food brings people together on many different levels. It's nourishment of the soul and body: it's truly love"
GIADA DE LAURENTIIS

"The nourishment of body is food, while the nourishment of the soul is feeding others"
ALI IBN ABI TALIB

"Nourishment is a factor which touches on the fundamental right to life"
POPE BENEDICT XVI

SELF-CARE PLAN – NOURISHMENT

In this Book I do not mandate any specific or special dietary or nutritional requirements. You are on your own unique journey to find your true purpose and to live into your best life and it is important that you gift yourself time to discover what is best for you.

Balance and moderation are important, and this applies to how you treat your body. Your heart is a very finely tuned engine that powers your life. To keep it functioning at its best it is important that you fuel it properly and that means choosing a healthy diet that will empower you to live into your best life in all ways.

HEART HEALTHY FOODS

I invite you to look at the following list of heart healthy foods that I suggest that you consider being a regular part of your life. These healthy heart foods are not an exhaustive list of all the foods you can have, they are a little starter pack for you to consider when choosing how you want to live into your best life.

FRUITS AND VEGETABLES

Fruit and vegetables provide your body with a great source of vitamins and minerals especially vitamin C and beta-carotene. Your heart would especially welcome more spinach; broccoli; cauliflower; bok choy; tomato; arugula; red and green peppers; carrots and asparagus. So really try and include them in your diet. These fruits and vegetables provide antioxidants to your body and help to slow down, and even prevent, atherosclerosis by reducing plaque buildup in your arteries.

SOLUBLE FIBER

Soluble fiber that you find in oats; beans; berries and ground flaxseed can help reduce your low density lipoprotein (bad) cholesterol levels in your body. When you increase soluble fiber into your diet it helps your heart health by reducing your blood pressure and inflammation and studies have shown that it helps reduce incidences of coronary heart disease and cardiovascular disease.

♥ **Author's Heartnote:** I recommend that you consult your doctor and nutritionist if you have special dietary requirements. This section is about simply highlighting that your nutrition really matters, especially as it relates to your heart health. I invite you to consider the information and use it in a way that is complimentary to you and for you moving forward positively in your life.

OMEGA 3 FATTY ACIDS

Omega 3 fatty acids such as salmon; tuna; herring; sardines; walnuts; ground flaxseed; hemp seeds and chia seeds are a key structure of every cell wall you have and are also an important energy source for your heart and other major organs. When you consume Omega 3s in your diet you help reduce blood clots which in turn keeps the lining of your arteries smooth and free of damage as well as helping stop plaque from forming in your arteries.

NOT HEART HEALTHY

I invite you to look at some of the foods that are not healthy for your heart (Please note that these are not exhaustive lists but rather a simple guide to make you feel into what is important for you.)

TRANS FATS AND SATURATED FATS

Trans fats and saturated fats raise your LDL (bad) cholesterol whilst also reducing your HDL (good) cholesterol. These fats can be detrimental to your health and wellbeing. Foods like peanut butter; packaged biscuits and cookies; packaged cakes; donuts and muffins; fatty cuts of red meat (porterhouse, rib eye); any fried food; pork; lamb; poultry with skin; butter; cheese; whole fat dairy can cause cholesterol to build up in your arteries which increases your risk of heart disease and stroke. It is also associated with developing Type 2 diabetes.

SALT (THESE FOODS CONTAIN HIGH
AMOUNTS OF SODIUM)

High salt (sodium) consumption can raise your blood pressure and is a major risk factor for heart disease and stroke. It is important to be mindful about in what foods sodium is used

174

"Trans fats really are metabolic poison"
WALTER WILLETT

"A high functioning palate allows you to live without sugar and sale"
NANCY S. MURE

and in what levels. Foods such as cereal; condiments; sauces; sweets (like cookies and cakes) can contain very high levels of salt. So be mindful about this and act in a way that is best for you and your life.

SUGAR

Sugar and high fructose corn syrup are two of the main types of added sugar in your foods. Sugar can cause inflammation in your body. A diet with too much sugar can lead to you having chronic inflammation which can stress your heart and blood vessels and drastically increase your risk of heart disease. Foods such as soft drinks; fruit drinks; lollies/candy; cakes, cookies, and pies; ice cream; sweetened yogurt and milk; sweet breads and waffles are a few of the better-known culprits here. Again, just as the case with salt in your diet, be mindful about this and act in a way that is best for you and your life.

WEEKLY MEAL DIARY

I invite you to consider this simple weekly meal diary for you to use to start tracking what you are eating so you can have an indication of what is actually fueling your body and driving your heart. You can also use the meal diary as a meal planner as well.

	BREAKFAST	LUNCH	DINNER	SNACKS
Mon				
Tue				
Wed				
Thu				

Fri

Sat

Sun

176

*"Mindfulness isn't difficult, we just
need to remember to do it"*
SHARON SALTZBERG

*"Mindfulness is a way if befriending
ourselves and our experience"*
JON KABAT ZINN

*"Mindfulness - The change in our
lives begins with a change in our
minds. Destiny grows where your
focus flows"*
ADELE BASHEER

HEARTING QUESTIONS - NOURISHMENT

- *When you look at the effect that nourishment has on you and your wellbeing how does it make you feel?*

- *What is coming up for you?*

- *When was the last time you acknowledged how important nourishment is in your life?*

- *What would your life be like if you nourished yourself properly every day?*

- *Would you like to be at your optimum in your life?*

- *What is stopping you from nourishing yourself effectively every day?*

You have a choice to maintain your status quo or take action.
What 3 things will you do this week to gift yourself time to nourish yourself effectively, and who will you have to keep you accountable?

1.

2.

3.

Commit yourself to take action in this area of your life today and be accountable.

If you need extra encouragement then invite someone onto your team and bring them on your journey.

Who is your nourishment accountability partner?

SELF-CARE PLAN - SLEEP

Your self-care is very important and whilst your diet, nutrition, hydration and how you breathe impacts on the quality of life you have, your sleep also plays a pivotal role in how you function every day.

Your sleeping life is not just important for your energy levels it is critical for your heart health too. Sleep should not be viewed as a luxury for you as it is critical for your good health and sleep helps your body repair and heal itself

Over the past 50 years the average sleep duration for people has decreased by 1.5 to 2 hours per night. A lack of sleep can have significant impacts upon you and it is important to get enough sleep to help protect your heart. I invite you to consider some powerful insights into how sleep actually protects your heart:

- When you have good-quality sleep it decreases the work of your heart because your blood pressure and heart rate go down at night.
- When you are sleep-deprived you actually show less variability in your heart rate. This lack of variability means that instead of functioning normally your heart rate stays at a higher elevated level and this is potentially dangerous as it presents as 'heightened stress'.
- A lack of sleep can increase your insulin resistance which can be a significant risk factor for the development of type 2 diabetes and heart disease.

"Prioritising good sleep is prioritizing good self-love"
UNKNOWN

"Sleep is the best meditation"
DALAI LAMA

"Sleep is the golden chain that binds health and our bodies together"
THOMAS DEKKER

- When you have shortened sleep, it can:
  - increase your C-reactive Protein (CRP) which is released with stress and inflammation. When you have high CRP it is a major risk factor for cardiovascular and heart disease.
  - interfere with the regulation of your appetite and this can have the effect that you end up eating more, or eating foods that are less healthy for your heart.

WHAT CAN YOU DO TO GET BETTER SLEEP?

If you know that you do not get enough sleep or that you toss and turn at night you already know that your sleeplessness impacts on your health and wellbeing in every part of your life.

All of the scientific research shows that having an on-going sleep deficit can ultimately endanger your heart health. I invite you to choose to adopt some of the following practices to help you sleep and live into your best life:

- Establish, and keep, a regular sleep schedule. Go to bed at the same time each night and get up at the same time each morning, including on the weekends.
- If you suffer from allergies remove the carpets or vacuum them regularly and change bed sheets weekly so dust doesn't accumulate and bother you.
- Ensure you get enough natural light, especially earlier in the day. Get active, go outside and go for a walk.
- Take part in physical activity and try not to exercise a few hours before you go to sleep.
- Avoid artificial light from phones and computers, especially just before you actually go to bed.
- Use a blue light filter on your computer or phone.
- Do not eat or drink within a few hours of going to bed, especially alcohol and foods high in fat or sugar.
- Make your sure your bedroom is set up so that it is noise free, dark and conducive to you getting a good night sleep.

HEARTING QUESTIONS - SLEEP

- *When you look at the effect that sleep has on you and your wellbeing how does it make you feel?*

- *What is coming up for you?*

- *When was the last time you acknowledged how important sleep is in your life?*

- *What would your life be like if you rested and slept properly every night?*

- *Would you like to be at your optimum in your life?*

- *What is stopping you from resting and sleeping every night?*

You have a choice to maintain your status quo or take action.

What 3 things will you do this week to gift yourself time to rest and sleep effectively, and who will you have to keep you accountable?

1.

2.

3.

Commit yourself to take action in this area of your life today and be accountable.

If you need extra encouragement then invite someone onto your team and bring them on your journey.

Who is your rest and sleep accountability partner?

SELF-CARE PLAN – MINDFULNESS

Throughout this Book I have spoken about the head/heart connection and the importance of dropping out of your head and into your heart. We looked at *m*Braining and neurolinguistics and the importance language plays in your heart connection journey.

I now invite you on a beautiful little journey into mindfulness but don't let the description fool you, it's not solely related to your mind and your head.

Mindfulness is about learning how to be fully present and engaged in the moment and being aware of your thoughts and feelings without any distraction or judgment.

You do not seek to control your thoughts and feelings, you simply pay attention to what is happening in the moment. This means that you allow all of your thoughts and feelings to exist in that particular moment and observe them with compassion, awareness and no judgement.

Mindfulness is all about your intention and your ability to turn your focus towards what is happening in the present moment and embracing all of it with curiosity, openness and compassion. In order for you to have full and mindful experiences in the present moment, you must firstly comprehend that you can separate yourself from your thoughts.

MINDFULNESS – THE THREE ELEMENTS

Mindfulness comprises three distinct and important elements that you need to be fully aware of:

- Intention
- Attention
- Attitude

There are three key elements to being mindful.

Firstly, it is important to start your session with the intention to be mindful.

180

"Mindfulness isn't difficult. We just need to remember to do it"
SHARON SALTZBERG

"Be happy in the moment, that's enough. Each moment is all we need, not more"
MOTHER THERESA

"Look past your thoughts so you may drink the pure nectar of this moment"
RUMI

Secondly, it is critical that you pay attention to what your mind, body and spirit are telling you and listen and feel into your surroundings and space. Tune out the white noise and all accompanying distractions and focus on the current moment and being fully immersed and focused on just that moment.

Thirdly, it is vital that you keep a positive attitude in order to manifest the destination where your mind, body and spirit need to go. As you go about your day be mindful and pay attention to the attitudes you bring into all situations so you can have more positivity in your life.

WHY DO YOU NEED MINDFULNESS?

The primary need for mindfulness in your life is for you to be present in the moment. Every day of your life you spend countless hours either living in the past or are transfixed on your future and you miss everything that is in front of you right now.

Mindfulness will lower your stress levels and allow you to be more productive in every area of your life. Practicing mindfulness will increase your focus and significantly limit your distractions.

Mindfulness will also improve the five areas that constitute a healthy lifestyle:

- **Sleep** - calm your mind and you will fall asleep easier and on a more regular basis
- **Nutrition** - mindful eating will help you will focus on the nutrients you are consuming and you will eat less calories as you focus on each tasty and nutritious bite
- **Exercise and Breathing** - focus on your breath instead of the exercise and you will complete workouts in a better frame of mind
- **Relationship** – your situational awareness will increase exponentially and this will allow you to fully appreciate

"Mindfulness isn't difficult. We just need to remember to do it"
SHARON SALTZBERG

"Be happy in the moment, that's enough. Each moment is all we need, not more"
MOTHER THERESA

"Look past your thoughts so you may drink the pure nectar of this moment"
RUMI

181

what is actually happening in your relationships on a deeper level

- **Cognition** - your thinking and understanding will improve into a healthy, more positive light

THE 7 STEPS TO MINDFULNESS

1. **Mindful breathing** – take a few minutes to focus on your breathing. Inhaling through your nose for six seconds and exhaling through your mouth for six seconds.

2. **Awareness** – be fully aware of your surroundings and all activities you are involved in. Ask yourself:

   How does it make you feel?

   What sensations are you feeling?

   How can you improve your experience in this space?

3. **Single Focus** – concentrate on what is in front of you and what you are doing in that moment and on each thing, you need to do to complete the task you are undertaking. ONE task at a time! Not a multitude!

4. **Meditation** – get comfortable and shut your eyes and imagine a beautiful place that brings you joy and focus on that. Clear your mind and allow yourself to just breathe and exist in your joy space.

5. **Journaling** – your Heart Whispers are a really important exercise to do every day as well as acknowledging everything that you appreciate and are grateful for.

6. **Acceptance of yourself** – who are you really? Feel into your heart and discover who you are. Look in the mirror each day and affirm exactly who you are.

7. **No distractions** – no white noise in your vicinity. Turn off all electronic devices and immerse yourself in silence for at least 5 minutes with no expectations. Just BE.

WEEKLY MINDFULNESS TABLE

I invite you to use this daily Mindfulness table so you can track how you are being mindful during your day. If you choose to do this, then be honest and authentic because it will provide you with information as to how committed you are to living into your best life. The choice is yours.

MINDFULNESS ACTION	COMPLETED (YES/NO)
Mindful breathing	
Awareness	
Single Focus	
Meditation	
Journaling	
Acceptance of Self	
No Distractions	

HEARTING QUESTIONS - MINDFULNESS

- *When you look at the effect that mindfulness has on you and your wellbeing how does it make you feel?*

- *What is coming up for you?*

- *When was the last time you acknowledged how important mindfulness is in your life?*

- *What would your life be like if you practiced mindfulness every day?*

- *Would you like to be at your optimum in your life?*

> • *What is stopping you from being mindful every day?*
>
> You have a choice to maintain your status quo or take action.
>
> What 3 things will you do this week to gift yourself time to practice mindfulness effectively, and who will you have to keep you accountable?
>
> 1.
>
> 2.
>
> 3.
>
> Commit yourself to take action in this area of your life today and be accountable.
>
> If you need extra encouragement then invite someone onto your team and bring them on your journey.
>
> **Who is your mindfulness accountability partner?**

PART VI

YOUR 100 HIDDEN HEARTS

188

"Time has a wonderful way of showing what really matters"
UNKNOWN

"The way we spend our time defines who we are"
JONATHON ESTRIN

"Time is what we want most, but what we use worst"
WILLIAM PENN

When you were born imagine that a simple glass life jar was placed beside you and it is with you in spirit everywhere you go. Your life jar has 100 marbles in it, one for every year of your life.

As you know, there is no guarantee that you will live to 100, as many souls are taken far earlier than that. In fact, depending on where you live your chances are only around 1-3% with Japan currently at that upward mark.

Now imagine that the Universe removes a marble from your jar every year. On your journey of life, you also get the opportunity(s) to connect with your heart and discover your Hidden Heart.

You have the power within yourself to choose to be the best you can be and your jar of 100 Hidden Hearts has been designed to guide you to reconnect with your heart; to live into your best life, a life of compassion and purpose in alignment with your Hidden Heart.

It is your own life journey that you are creating and living into. The 100 Hidden Hearts are yours, every marble represents a year of your life and every year you gift yourself the opportunity to connect with your hidden heart and live a beautiful compassionate heart filled life … or not!

The choice is yours.

It is exciting to know that you have the choice, right now to connect with your heart and this Book is your personal guide on how to do it. I invite you to take the opportunity to journey within and really make the most of your time here on earth.

In this section of the Book, you will see your life clock right before your eyes. Every year from your birth to 100 years is represented and you can start to interact and feel into every year with a new heart-based connection.

Every seven years you will be invited to complete a seven-year review of your life. It is a scientifically proven fact, according to Rudolf Steiner and other scientists that seven-year cycles are extremely important. This is because our minds and bodies literally change at a cellular level every seven years.

In your Hidden Heart Journey, you will be given the opportunity to feel into your heart and reflect on your life as it evolved and transformed over your previous seven years.

What was your life theme?

What were your key learnings?

How are you living into your best life?

How will your next seven years be transformative for you?

♥ **Author's Heartnote:** In the following Hidden Heart marble pages there is a basic and yet confronting life countdown clock. This clock contains information about the hours, days, months, and years of your life, if, you live to 100. You may also notice that your clock does not include leap years. It has been kept very simple to convey an underlying message: make the most of every second of your life.

BIRTH YEAR – 100 MARBLES IN YOUR LIFE JAR

A year of your life has already passed, and the hours, days, months, and years of your existence will not be gifted back.

YOUR HIDDEN HEARTLINES
This is how much time you have already used in your life:

MONTHS	DAYS	HOURS
12	365	8,760

This is how much time you have in your life **if** you live to 100.

MONTHS	DAYS	HOURS
1200	36,500	876,000

YEAR 1 – 99 MARBLES IN YOUR LIFE JAR

Another year of your life has passed, and the hours, days, months, and years of your existence will not be gifted back.

YOUR HIDDEN HEARTLINES
This is how much time you have already used in your life:

MONTHS	DAYS	HOURS
24	730	17,520

This is how much time you have in your life **if** you live to 100:

MONTHS	DAYS	HOURS
1188	36,135	867,240

190 *"All we have to decide is what to do with the time that is given us"*
J.R.R. TOLKEIN

"An inch of time is an inch of gold, but you can't buy that inch of time with an inch of gold"
CHINESE PROVERB

"The two most powerful warriors are patience and time"
LEO TOLSTOY

"A man who dares to waste one hour of time has not discovered the value of life"
CHARLES DARWIN

YEAR 2 - 98 MARBLES IN YOUR LIFE JAR

Another year of your life has passed, and the hours, days, months, and years of your existence will not be gifted back.

YOUR HIDDEN HEARTLINES

This is how much time you have already used in your life:

MONTHS	DAYS	HOURS
36	1095	26,280

This is how much time you have in your life **if** you live to 100:

MONTHS	DAYS	HOURS
1176	35,770	1176

YEAR 3 - 97 MARBLES IN YOUR LIFE JAR

Another year of your life has passed, and the hours, days, months, and years of your existence will not be gifted back.

YOUR HIDDEN HEARTLINES

This is how much time you have already used in your life:

MONTHS	DAYS	HOURS
48	1460	35,040

This is how much time you have in your life **if** you live to 100:

MONTHS	DAYS	HOURS
1164	35,405	849,720

Your Hidden Heart Diamond

It is time for you to reflect on your life journey this year and truly feel into your heartspace. Have I been connected to Source? Have I been connected to my Inner Child? Have I been connected to my Heart? Have I been connected to my Life Purpose? Have I recognised and been managing my Ego? What is my Hidden Heart?

Your Hidden Heart Year Ahead

It is important that you not only reflect on the year that has passed but it is critical that you also feel into your future year ahead. I invite you to gift yourself the time to complete your Heart Existence Mirror and your Future Heart Map and use these to help guide you on your journey towards your Hidden Heart.

YEAR 4 - 96 MARBLES IN YOUR LIFE JAR

Another year of your life has passed, and the hours, days, months, and years of your existence will not be gifted back.

YOUR HIDDEN HEARTLINES
This is how much time you have already used in your life:

MONTHS	DAYS	HOURS
60	1825	43,800

This is how much time you have in your life **if** you live to 100:

MONTHS	DAYS	HOURS
1152	35,040	840,960

YEAR 5 - 95 MARBLES IN YOUR LIFE JAR

Another year of your life has passed, and the hours, days, months, and years of your existence will not be gifted back.

YOUR HIDDEN HEARTLINES
This is how much time you have already used in your life:

MONTHS	DAYS	HOURS
72	2190	52,560

This is how much time you have in your life **if** you live to 100:

MONTHS	DAYS	HOURS
1140	34,675	832,200

YEAR 6 - 94 MARBLES IN YOUR LIFE JAR

Another year of your life has passed, and the hours, days, months, and years of your existence will not be gifted back.

YOUR HIDDEN HEARTLINES

This is how much time you have already used in your life:

MONTHS	DAYS	HOURS
84	2,555	61,320

This is how much time you have in your life **if** you live to 100:

MONTHS	DAYS	HOURS
1128	34,310	823,440

Your Hidden Heart Diamond

It is time for you to reflect on your life journey this year and truly feel into your heartspace. Have I been connected to Source? Have I been connected to my Inner Child? Have I been connected to my Heart? Have I been connected to my Life Purpose? Have I recognised and been managing my Ego? What is my Hidden Heart?

Your Hidden Heart Year Ahead

It is important that you not only reflect on the year that has passed but it is critical that you also feel into your future year ahead. I invite you to gift yourself the time to complete your Heart Existence Mirror and your Future Heart Map and use these to help guide you on your journey towards your Hidden Heart.

194 ♥ **Author's Heartnote:** It is important to note that when you feel into your heart and reflect over your past seven years there may be significant feelings and emotions that are released, and you need to create a safe space for yourself to heal and grow if this eventuates. If you feel overwhelmed, it is critical that you seek appropriate help and support.

"Your time is limited so don't waste it living someone else's life"
STEVE JOBS

"Time is what we want most but use worst"
WILLIAM PENN

YOUR SEVEN YEAR HIDDEN HEART LIFE REVIEW

YOUR HIDDEN HEART DIAMOND

How was your connection with Source?

How was your connection with your inner child?

How was your connection with your heart?

How was your connection with your life purpose?

Where was your Ego?

What was your Hidden Heart?

YOUR LIFE JOURNEY

What was your life theme?

What were key heart learnings?

How are you living into my best life now?

What was your greatest achievement from the past seven years? Why do you consider it your greatest achievement?

What was your greatest surprise of the past seven years?

What did you set out to achieve over the past seven years but haven't accomplished it yet?

How will your next seven years be transformative for you?

What do you plan to do to celebrate your beautiful successes over the past seven Years?

What is your legacy gift?

YEAR 7 - 93 MARBLES IN YOUR LIFE JAR

Another year of your life has passed, and the hours, days, months, and years of your existence will not be gifted back.

YOUR HIDDEN HEARTLINES
This is how much time you have already used in your life:

MONTHS	DAYS	HOURS
96	2,920	70,080

This is how much time you have in your life **if** you live to 100:

MONTHS	DAYS	HOURS
1116	33,945	814,680

YEAR 8 - 92 MARBLES IN YOUR LIFE JAR

Another year of your life has passed, and the hours, days, months, and years of your existence will not be gifted back.

YOUR HIDDEN HEARTLINES
This is how much time you have already used in your life:

MONTHS	DAYS	HOURS
108	3,285	78,840

This is how much time you have in your life **if** you live to 100:

MONTHS	DAYS	HOURS
1104	33,508	805,920

Your Hidden Heart Diamond
It is time for you to reflect on your life journey this year and truly feel into your heartspace. Have I been connected to Source? Have I been connected to my Inner Child? Have I been connected to my Heart? Have I been connected to my Life Purpose? Have I recognised and been managing my Ego? What is my Hidden Heart?

Your Hidden Heart Year Ahead
It is important that you not only reflect on the year that has passed but it is critical that you also feel into your future year ahead. I invite you to gift yourself the time to complete your Heart Existence Mirror and your Future Heart Map and use these to help guide you on your journey towards your Hidden Heart.

YEAR 9 - 91 MARBLES IN YOUR LIFE JAR

Another year of your life has passed, and the hours, days, months, and years of your existence will not be gifted back.

MY HIDDEN HEARTLINES
This is how much time you have already used in your life:

MONTHS	DAYS	HOURS
120	3,650	87,600

This is how much time you have in your life **if** you live to 100:

MONTHS	DAYS	HOURS
1092	33,215	797,160

"Never give up because great things take time"
UNKNOWN

"Never stop learning because life never stops teaching"
UNKNOWN

"Good things take time"
UNKNOWN

"Life is not a problem to be solved, but a reality to be experienced"
SOREN KIERKIGAARD

YEAR 10 - 90 MARBLES IN YOUR LIFE JAR

Another year of your life has passed, and the hours, days, months, and years of your existence will not be gifted back.

MY HIDDEN HEARTLINES
This is how much time you have already used in your life:

MONTHS	DAYS	HOURS
132	4,015	96,360

This is how much time you have in your life **if** you live to 100:

MONTHS	DAYS	HOURS
1080	32,850	788,400

YEAR 11 - 89 MARBLES IN YOUR LIFE JAR

Another year of your life has passed, and the hours, days, months, and years of your existence will not be gifted back.

MY HIDDEN HEARTLINES
This is how much time you have already used in your life:

MONTHS	DAYS	HOURS
144	4,380	105,120

This is how much time you have in your life **if** you live to 100:

MONTHS	DAYS	HOURS
1068	32,485	779,640

Your Hidden Heart Diamond   *197*
It is time for you to reflect on your life journey this year and truly feel into your heartspace. Have I been connected to Source? Have I been connected to my Inner Child? Have I been connected to my Heart? Have I been connected to my Life Purpose? Have I recognised and been managing my Ego? What is my Hidden Heart?

Your Hidden Heart Year Ahead
It is important that you not only reflect on the year that has passed but it is critical that you also feel into your future year ahead. I invite you to gift yourself the time to complete your Heart Existence Mirror and your Future Heart Map and use these to help guide you on your journey towards your Hidden Heart.

YEAR 12 - 88 MARBLES IN YOUR LIFE JAR

Another year of your life has passed, and the hours, days, months, and years of your existence will not be gifted back.

MY HIDDEN HEARTLINES
This is how much time you have already used in your life:

MONTHS	DAYS	HOURS
156	4,745	113,880

This is how much time you have in your life **if** you live to 100:

MONTHS	DAYS	HOURS
1056	32,120	770,880

YEAR 13 - 87 MARBLES IN YOUR LIFE JAR

Another year of your life has passed, and the hours, days, months, and years of your existence will not be gifted back.

MY HIDDEN HEARTLINES
This is how much time you have already used in your life:

MONTHS	DAYS	HOURS
168	5,110	122,640

This is how much time you have in your life **if** you live to 100:

MONTHS	DAYS	HOURS
1104	31,755	762,120

"A thousand words will not leave so deep an impression as one deed"
HENRIK IBSEN

YOUR SEVEN YEAR HIDDEN HEART LIFE REVIEW

YOUR HIDDEN HEART DIAMOND

How was your connection with Source?

How was your connection with your inner child?

How was your connection with your heart?

How was your connection with your life purpose?

Where was your Ego?

What was your Hidden Heart?

YOUR LIFE JOURNEY

What was your life theme?

What were key heart learnings?

How are you living into my best life now?

What was your greatest achievement from the past seven years? Why do you consider it your greatest achievement?

What was your greatest surprise of the past seven years?

What did you set out to achieve over the past seven years but haven't accomplished it yet?

How will your next seven years be transformative for you?

What do you plan to do to celebrate your beautiful successes over the past seven Years?

What is your legacy gift?

♥ **Author's Heartnote:** It is important to note that when you feel into your heart and reflect over your past seven years there may be significant feelings and emotions that are released, and you need to create a safe space for yourself to heal and grow if this eventuates. If you feel overwhelmed, it is critical that you seek appropriate help and support.

YEAR 14 - 86 MARBLES IN YOUR LIFE JAR

Another year of your life has passed, and the hours, days, months, and years of your existence will not be gifted back.

MY HIDDEN HEARTLINES
This is how much time you have already used in your life:

MONTHS	DAYS	HOURS
180	5,475	131,400

This is how much time you have in your life **if** you live to 100:

MONTHS	DAYS	HOURS
1032	31,390	753,360

200 *"Don't wait. The time will never be just right"*
NAPOLEON HILL

"Everything you want is on the other side of fear"
JACK CANFIELD

"It is never TOO LATE to be what you might have been"
GEORGE ELIOT

"Be someone's strength. Be someone's inspiration. Be someone's reason to never give up"
UNKNOWN

YEAR 15 - 85 MARBLES IN YOUR LIFE JAR

Another year of your life has passed, and the hours, days, months, and years of your existence will not be gifted back.

MY HIDDEN HEARTLINES
This is how much time you have already used in your life:

MONTHS	DAYS	HOURS
195	5,840	140,160

This is how much time you have in your life **if** you live to 100:

MONTHS	DAYS	HOURS
1020	31,025	744,600

YEAR 16 - 84 MARBLES IN YOUR LIFE JAR

Another year of your life has passed, and the hours, days, months, and years of your existence will not be gifted back.

MY HIDDEN HEARTLINES
This is how much time you have already used in your life:

MONTHS	DAYS	HOURS
204	6,205	148,920

This is how much time you have in your life **if** you live to 100:

MONTHS	DAYS	HOURS
1008	30,660	735,840

YEAR 17 - 83 MARBLES IN YOUR LIFE JAR

Another year of your life has passed, and the hours, days, months, and years of your existence will not be gifted back.

MY HIDDEN HEARTLINES
This is how much time you have already used in your life:

MONTHS	DAYS	HOURS
216	6,570	157,680

This is how much time you have in your life **if** you live to 100:

MONTHS	DAYS	HOURS
996	30,295	727,080

Your Hidden Heart Diamond

It is time for you to reflect on your life journey this year and truly feel into your heartspace. Have I been connected to Source? Have I been connected to my Inner Child? Have I been connected to my Heart? Have I been connected to my Life Purpose? Have I recognised and been managing my Ego? What is my Hidden Heart?

Your Hidden Heart Year Ahead

It is important that you not only reflect on the year that has passed but it is critical that you also feel into your future year ahead. I invite you to gift yourself the time to complete your Heart Existence Mirror and your Future Heart Map and use these to help guide you on your journey towards your Hidden Heart.

YEAR 18 - 82 MARBLES IN YOUR LIFE JAR

Another year of your life has passed, and the hours, days, months, and years of your existence will not be gifted back.

MY HIDDEN HEARTLINES
This is how much time you have already used in your life:

MONTHS	DAYS	HOURS
228	6,935	166,440

This is how much time you have in your life **if** you live to 100:

MONTHS	DAYS	HOURS
984	29,930	718,320

202

"Sometimes you will never know the value of a moment until it becomes a memory"
DR SEUSS

"Let your dreams be your wings"
UNKNOWN

"Time is a created thing. To say, I don't have time, is to say I don't want to"
LAO TZU

YEAR 19 - 81 MARBLES IN YOUR LIFE JAR

Another year of your life has passed, and the hours, days, months, and years of your existence will not be gifted back.

MY HIDDEN HEARTLINES
This is how much time you have already used in your life:

MONTHS	DAYS	HOURS
240	7,300	175,200

This is how much time you have in your life **if** you live to 100:

MONTHS	DAYS	HOURS
972	29,565	709,560

YEAR 20 - 80 MARBLES IN YOUR LIFE JAR

Another year of your life has passed, and the hours, days, months, and years of your existence will not be gifted back.

MY HIDDEN HEARTLINES
This is how much time you have already used in your life:

MONTHS	DAYS	HOURS
252	7,665	183,960

This is how much time you have in your life **if** you live to 100:

MONTHS	DAYS	HOURS
960	29,200	700,800

Your Hidden Heart Diamond
It is time for you to reflect on your life journey this year and truly feel into your heartspace. Have I been connected to Source? Have I been connected to my Inner Child? Have I been connected to my Heart? Have I been connected to my Life Purpose? Have I recognised and been managing my Ego? What is my Hidden Heart?

Your Hidden Heart Year Ahead
It is important that you not only reflect on the year that has passed but it is critical that you also feel into your future year ahead. I invite you to gift yourself the time to complete your Heart Existence Mirror and your Future Heart Map and use these to help guide you on your journey towards your Hidden Heart.

204 ♥ **Author's Heartnote:** It is important to note that when you feel into your heart and reflect over your past seven years there may be significant feelings and emotions that are released, and you need to create a safe space for yourself to heal and grow if this eventuates. If you feel overwhelmed, it is critical that you seek appropriate help and support.

"Your only limit ... is YOU!"
UNKNOWN

"If you carry joy in your heart, you can heal any moment"
CARLOS SANTANA

YOUR SEVEN YEAR HIDDEN HEART LIFE REVIEW

YOUR HIDDEN HEART DIAMOND

How was your connection with Source?

How was your connection with your inner child?

How was your connection with your heart?

How was your connection with your life purpose?

Where was your Ego?

What was your Hidden Heart?

YOUR LIFE JOURNEY

What was your life theme?

What were key heart learnings?

How are you living into my best life now?

What was your greatest achievement from the past seven years? Why do you consider it your greatest achievement?

What was your greatest surprise of the past seven years?

What did you set out to achieve over the past seven years but haven't accomplished it yet?

How will your next seven years be transformative for you?

What do you plan to do to celebrate your beautiful successes over the past seven Years?

What is your legacy gift?

YEAR 21 - 79 MARBLES IN YOUR LIFE JAR

Another year of your life has passed, and the hours, days, months, and years of your existence will not be gifted back.

MY HIDDEN HEARTLINES
This is how much time you have already used in your life:

MONTHS	DAYS	HOURS
264	8,030	192,720

This is how much time you have in your life **if** you live to 100:

MONTHS	DAYS	HOURS
948	28,835	692,040

YEAR 22 - 78 MARBLES IN YOUR LIFE JAR

Another year of your life has passed, and the hours, days, months, and years of your existence will not be gifted back.

MY HIDDEN HEARTLINES
This is how much time you have already used in your life:

MONTHS	DAYS	HOURS
276	8,395	201,480

This is how much time you have in your life **if** you live to 100:

MONTHS	DAYS	HOURS
936	28,470	683,280

Your Hidden Heart Diamond

It is time for you to reflect on your life journey this year and truly feel into your heartspace. Have I been connected to Source? Have I been connected to my Inner Child? Have I been connected to my Heart? Have I been connected to my Life Purpose? Have I recognised and been managing my Ego? What is my Hidden Heart?

Your Hidden Heart Year Ahead

It is important that you not only reflect on the year that has passed but it is critical that you also feel into your future year ahead. I invite you to gift yourself the time to complete your Heart Existence Mirror and your Future Heart Map and use these to help guide you on your journey towards your Hidden Heart.

YEAR 23 - 77 MARBLES IN YOUR LIFE JAR

Another year of your life has passed, and the hours, days, months, and years of your existence will not be gifted back.

MY HIDDEN HEARTLINES
This is how much time you have already used in your life:

MONTHS	DAYS	HOURS
288	8,760	210,240

This is how much time you have in your life **if** you live to 100:

MONTHS	DAYS	HOURS
924	28,105	674,520

"Your future needs you. Your past doesn't!"
UNKNOWN

"If you want to achieve greatness stop asking for permission"
UNKNOWN

"If you want to fly give up everything that weighs you down"
BUDDHA

"Sometimes we are tested not to show our weaknesses, but to show our strengths"
UNKNOWN

YEAR 24 - 76 MARBLES IN YOUR LIFE JAR

Another year of your life has passed, and the hours, days, months, and years of your existence will not be gifted back.

MY HIDDEN HEARTLINES
This is how much time you have already used in your life:

MONTHS	DAYS	HOURS
300	9,125	219,00

This is how much time you have in your life **if** you live to 100:

MONTHS	DAYS	HOURS
912	27,740	665,760

YEAR 25 - 75 MARBLES IN YOUR LIFE JAR

Another year of your life has passed, and the hours, days, months, and years of your existence will not be gifted back.

MY HIDDEN HEARTLINES
This is how much time you have already used in your life:

MONTHS	DAYS	HOURS
312	9,490	227,760

This is how much time you have in your life **if** you live to 100:

MONTHS	DAYS	HOURS
900	27,375	657,000

YEAR 26 - 74 MARBLES IN YOUR LIFE JAR

Another year of your life has passed, and the hours, days, months, and years of your existence will not be gifted back.

MY HIDDEN HEARTLINES
This is how much time you have already used in your life:

MONTHS	DAYS	HOURS
324	9,855	236,520

This is how much time you have in your life **if** you live to 100:

MONTHS	DAYS	HOURS
888	27,010	648,240

Your Hidden Heart Diamond
It is time for you to reflect on your life journey this year and truly feel into your heartspace. Have I been connected to Source? Have I been connected to my Inner Child? Have I been connected to my Heart? Have I been connected to my Life Purpose? Have I recognised and been managing my Ego? What is my Hidden Heart?

Your Hidden Heart Year Ahead
It is important that you not only reflect on the year that has passed but it is critical that you also feel into your future year ahead. I invite you to gift yourself the time to complete your Heart Existence Mirror and your Future Heart Map and use these to help guide you on your journey towards your Hidden Heart.

YEAR 27 - 73 MARBLES IN YOUR LIFE JAR

Another year of your life has passed, and the hours, days, months, and years of your existence will not be gifted back.

MY HIDDEN HEARTLINES
This is how much time you have already used in your life:

MONTHS	DAYS	HOURS
336	10,220	245,280

208   *"Life begins at the end of your comfort zone"*
NEALE DONALD WALSH

This is how much time you have in your life **if** you live to 100:

MONTHS	DAYS	HOURS
876	26,645	639,480

YOUR SEVEN YEAR HIDDEN HEART LIFE REVIEW

♥ **Author's Heartnote:** It is *209*
important to note that when you feel
into your heart and reflect over your
past seven years there may be signif-
icant feelings and emotions that are
released, and you need to create a
safe space for yourself to heal and
grow if this eventuates. If you feel
overwhelmed, it is critical that you
seek appropriate help and support.

YOUR HIDDEN HEART DIAMOND

How was your connection with Source?

How was your connection with your inner child?

How was your connection with your heart?

How was your connection with your life purpose?

Where was your Ego?

What was your Hidden Heart?

YOUR LIFE JOURNEY

What was your life theme?

What were key heart learnings?

How are you living into my best life now?

What was your greatest achievement from the past seven
years? Why do you consider it your greatest achievement?

What was your greatest surprise of the past seven years?

What did you set out to achieve over the past seven years but
haven't accomplished it yet?

How will your next seven years be transformative for you?

What do you plan to do to celebrate your beautiful successes
over the past seven Years?

What is your legacy gift?

YEAR 28 - 72 MARBLES IN YOUR LIFE JAR

Another year of your life has passed, and the hours, days, months, and years of your existence will not be gifted back.

MY HIDDEN HEARTLINES
This is how much time you have already used in your life:

MONTHS	DAYS	HOURS
348	1,585	254,040

This is how much time you have in your life **if** you live to 100:

MONTHS	DAYS	HOURS
864	26,280	360,720

210   *"Everyone sees what you appear to be, few experience what you truly are"*
UNKNOWN

"A year from now you may wish you had started today"
KAREN LAMB

"Do not be afraid to fail. Be afraid not to even try!"
UNKNOWN

"If my life is going to mean anything, I have to live it myself"
RICK RIORDAN

YEAR 29 - 71 MARBLES IN YOUR LIFE JAR

Another year of your life has passed, and the hours, days, months, and years of your existence will not be gifted back.

MY HIDDEN HEARTLINES
This is how much time you have already used in your life:

MONTHS	DAYS	HOURS
360	10,950	262,800

This is how much time you have in your life **if** you live to 100:

MONTHS	DAYS	HOURS
852	25,915	621,960

YEAR 30 - 70 MARBLES IN YOUR LIFE JAR

Another year of your life has passed, and the hours, days, months, and years of your existence will not be gifted back.

MY HIDDEN HEARTLINES

This is how much time you have already used in your life:

MONTHS	DAYS	HOURS
372	11,315	271,560

This is how much time you have in your life **if** you live to 100:

MONTHS	DAYS	HOURS
840	25,550	613,200

YEAR 31 - 69 MARBLES IN YOUR LIFE JAR

Another year of your life has passed, and the hours, days, months, and years of your existence will not be gifted back.

MY HIDDEN HEARTLINES

This is how much time you have already used in your life:

MONTHS	DAYS	HOURS
384	11,680	280,320

This is how much time you have in your life **if** you live to 100:

MONTHS	DAYS	HOURS
828	25,185	604,440

Your Hidden Heart Diamond

It is time for you to reflect on your life journey this year and truly feel into your heartspace. Have I been connected to Source? Have I been connected to my Inner Child? Have I been connected to my Heart? Have I been connected to my Life Purpose? Have I recognised and been managing my Ego? What is my Hidden Heart?

Your Hidden Heart Year Ahead

It is important that you not only reflect on the year that has passed but it is critical that you also feel into your future year ahead. I invite you to gift yourself the time to complete your Heart Existence Mirror and your Future Heart Map and use these to help guide you on your journey towards your Hidden Heart.

YEAR 32 - 68 MARBLES IN YOUR LIFE JAR

Another year of your life has passed, and the hours, days, months, and years of your existence will not be gifted back.

MY HIDDEN HEARTLINES
This is how much time you have already used in your life:

MONTHS	DAYS	HOURS
396	12,045	289,680

This is how much time you have in your life **if** you live to 100:

MONTHS	DAYS	HOURS
816	24,820	595,680

YEAR 33 - 67 MARBLES IN YOUR LIFE JAR

Another year of your life has passed, and the hours, days, months, and years of your existence will not be gifted back.

MY HIDDEN HEARTLINES
This is how much time you have already used in your life:

MONTHS	DAYS	HOURS
408	12,410	297,840

This is how much time you have in your life **if** you live to 100:

MONTHS	DAYS	HOURS
804	24,455	586,920

YEAR 34 - 66 MARBLES IN YOUR LIFE JAR

Another year of your life has passed, and the hours, days, months, and years of your existence will not be gifted back.

MY HIDDEN HEARTLINES
This is how much time you have already used in your life:

MONTHS	DAYS	HOURS
420	12,775	306,600

This is how much time you have in your life **if** you live to 100:

MONTHS	DAYS	HOURS
792	24,090	578,160

Your Hidden Heart Diamond
It is time for you to reflect on your life journey this year and truly feel into your heartspace. Have I been connected to Source? Have I been connected to my Inner Child? Have I been connected to my Heart? Have I been connected to my Life Purpose? Have I recognised and been managing my Ego? What is my Hidden Heart?

Your Hidden Heart Year Ahead
It is important that you not only reflect on the year that has passed but it is critical that you also feel into your future year ahead. I invite you to gift yourself the time to complete your Heart Existence Mirror and your Future Heart Map and use these to help guide you on your journey towards your Hidden Heart.

214 ♥ **Author's Heartnote:** It is important to note that when you feel into your heart and reflect over your past seven years there may be significant feelings and emotions that are released, and you need to create a safe space for yourself to heal and grow if this eventuates. If you feel overwhelmed, it is critical that you seek appropriate help and support.

"Nothing is impossible. The word itself says I'm Possible!"
AUDREY HEPBURN

"You will truly never be good enough for anyone else, if you are not good enough for yourself first!"
UNKNOWN

YOUR SEVEN YEAR HIDDEN HEART LIFE REVIEW

YOUR HIDDEN HEART DIAMOND

How was your connection with Source?

How was your connection with your inner child?

How was your connection with your heart?

How was your connection with your life purpose?

Where was your Ego?

What was your Hidden Heart?

YOUR LIFE JOURNEY

What was your life theme?

What were key heart learnings?

How are you living into my best life now?

What was your greatest achievement from the past seven years? Why do you consider it your greatest achievement?

What was your greatest surprise of the past seven years?

What did you set out to achieve over the past seven years but haven't accomplished it yet?

How will your next seven years be transformative for you?

What do you plan to do to celebrate your beautiful successes over the past seven Years?

What is your legacy gift?

YEAR 35 - 65 MARBLES IN YOUR LIFE JAR

Another year of your life has passed, and the hours, days, months, and years of your existence will not be gifted back.

MY HIDDEN HEARTLINES
This is how much time you have already used in your life:

MONTHS	DAYS	HOURS
432	13,140	315,360

This is how much time you have in your life **if** you live to 100:

MONTHS	DAYS	HOURS
780	23,725	569,400

YEAR 36 - 64 MARBLES IN YOUR LIFE JAR

Another year of your life has passed, and the hours, days, months, and years of your existence will not be gifted back.

MY HIDDEN HEARTLINES
This is how much time you have already used in your life:

MONTHS	DAYS	HOURS
444	13,505	324,120

This is how much time you have in your life **if** you live to 100:

MONTHS	DAYS	HOURS
768	23,360	560,640

Your Hidden Heart Diamond
It is time for you to reflect on your life journey this year and truly feel into your heartspace. Have I been connected to Source? Have I been connected to my Inner Child? Have I been connected to my Heart? Have I been connected to my Life Purpose? Have I recognised and been managing my Ego? What is my Hidden Heart?

Your Hidden Heart Year Ahead
It is important that you not only reflect on the year that has passed but it is critical that you also feel into your future year ahead. I invite you to gift yourself the time to complete your Heart Existence Mirror and your Future Heart Map and use these to help guide you on your journey towards your Hidden Heart.

YEAR 37 - 63 MARBLES IN YOUR LIFE JAR

Another year of your life has passed, and the hours, days, months, and years of your existence will not be gifted back.

MY HIDDEN HEARTLINES
This is how much time you have already used in your life:

MONTHS	DAYS	HOURS
456	13,870	332,880

This is how much time you have in your life **if** you live to 100:

MONTHS	DAYS	HOURS
756	22,995	551,880

216   *"And those who were seen dancing were thought to be insane by those who could not hear the music!"*
FREDERICH NEITZSCHE

"Believe in yourself and you will be unstoppable!"
UNKNOWN

"It is not the mountain we conquer, but ourselves"
SIR EDMUND HILLARY

"We rise by lifting others"
UNKNOWN

YEAR 38 - 62 MARBLES IN YOUR LIFE JAR

Another year of your life has passed, and the hours, days, months, and years of your existence will not be gifted back.

MY HIDDEN HEARTLINES
This is how much time you have already used in your life:

MONTHS	DAYS	HOURS
468	14,235	341,640

This is how much time you have in your life **if** you live to 100:

MONTHS	DAYS	HOURS
744	22,630	543,120

YEAR 39 - 61 MARBLES IN YOUR LIFE JAR

Another year of your life has passed, and the hours, days, months, and years of your existence will not be gifted back.

MY HIDDEN HEARTLINES
This is how much time you have already used in your life:

MONTHS	DAYS	HOURS
480	14,600	350,400

This is how much time you have in your life **if** you live to 100:

MONTHS	DAYS	HOURS
732	22,265	534,360

YEAR 40 - 60 MARBLES IN YOUR LIFE JAR

Another year of your life has passed, and the hours, days, months, and years of your existence will not be gifted back.

MY HIDDEN HEARTLINES
This is how much time you have already used in your life:

MONTHS	DAYS	HOURS
492	14,965	359,160

This is how much time you have in your life **if** you live to 100:

MONTHS	DAYS	HOURS
720	21,900	525,600

Your Hidden Heart Diamond
It is time for you to reflect on your life journey this year and truly feel into your heartspace. Have I been connected to Source? Have I been connected to my Inner Child? Have I been connected to my Heart? Have I been connected to my Life Purpose? Have I recognised and been managing my Ego? What is my Hidden Heart?

Your Hidden Heart Year Ahead
It is important that you not only reflect on the year that has passed but it is critical that you also feel into your future year ahead. I invite you to gift yourself the time to complete your Heart Existence Mirror and your Future Heart Map and use these to help guide you on your journey towards your Hidden Heart.

YEAR 41 - 59 MARBLES IN YOUR LIFE JAR

Another year of your life has passed, and the hours, days, months, and years of your existence will not be gifted back.

MY HIDDEN HEARTLINES
This is how much time you have already used in your life:

MONTHS	DAYS	HOURS
504	15,330	367,920

This is how much time you have in your life **if** you live to 100:

MONTHS	DAYS	HOURS
708	21,535	516,840

218 *"Be the reason someone smiles today"*
UNKNOWN

YOUR SEVEN YEAR HIDDEN HEART LIFE REVIEW

♥ **Author's Heartnote:** It is 219 important to note that when you feel into your heart and reflect over your past seven years there may be significant feelings and emotions that are released, and you need to create a safe space for yourself to heal and grow if this eventuates. If you feel overwhelmed, it is critical that you seek appropriate help and support.

YOUR HIDDEN HEART DIAMOND

How was your connection with Source?

How was your connection with your inner child?

How was your connection with your heart?

How was your connection with your life purpose?

Where was your Ego?

What was your Hidden Heart?

YOUR LIFE JOURNEY

What was your life theme?

What were key heart learnings?

How are you living into my best life now?

What was your greatest achievement from the past seven years? Why do you consider it your greatest achievement?

What was your greatest surprise of the past seven years?

What did you set out to achieve over the past seven years but haven't accomplished it yet?

How will your next seven years be transformative for you?

What do you plan to do to celebrate your beautiful successes over the past seven Years?

What is your legacy gift?

YEAR 42 - 58 MARBLES IN YOUR LIFE JAR

Another year of your life has passed, and the hours, days, months, and years of your existence will not be gifted back.

MY HIDDEN HEARTLINES
This is how much time you have already used in your life:

MONTHS	DAYS	HOURS
516	15,695	376,680

This is how much time you have in your life **if** you live to 100:

MONTHS	DAYS	HOURS
696	21,170	508,080

220 *"Never apologise for being sensitive or emotional. Let this be a sign that you have got a big heart and are not afraid to let others see it. Showing your emotions is a sign of strength"*
BRIGITTE NICOLE

"Follow your heart, listen to your inner voice, stop caring about what others think"
JIMMI HENDRIX

"If you want to build a ship, don't drum up the men to gather wood, divide the work and give orders. Instead, teach them to yearn for the vast and endless sea"
ANTOINE DE SAINT EXUPERY

"Never give up on anything that makes your heart soar"
UNKNOWN

YEAR 43 - 57 MARBLES IN YOUR LIFE JAR

Another year of your life has passed, and the hours, days, months, and years of your existence will not be gifted back.

MY HIDDEN HEARTLINES
This is how much time you have already used in your life:

MONTHS	DAYS	HOURS
528	16,060	385,440

This is how much time you have in your life **if** you live to 100:

MONTHS	DAYS	HOURS
684	20,805	499,320

YEAR 44 - 56 MARBLES IN YOUR LIFE JAR

Another year of your life has passed, and the hours, days, months, and years of your existence will not be gifted back.

MY HIDDEN HEARTLINES
This is how much time you have already used in your life:

MONTHS	DAYS	HOURS
540	16,425	394,200

This is how much time you have in your life **if** you live to 100:

MONTHS	DAYS	HOURS
672	20,440	490,560

YEAR 45 - 55 MARBLES IN YOUR LIFE JAR

Another year of your life has passed, and the hours, days, months, and years of your existence will not be gifted back.

MY HIDDEN HEARTLINES
This is how much time you have already used in your life:

MONTHS	DAYS	HOURS
552	16,790	402,960

This is how much time you have in your life **if** you live to 100:

MONTHS	DAYS	HOURS
660	20,075	481,800

Your Hidden Heart Diamond
It is time for you to reflect on your life journey this year and truly feel into your heartspace. Have I been connected to Source? Have I been connected to my Inner Child? Have I been connected to my Heart? Have I been connected to my Life Purpose? Have I recognised and been managing my Ego? What is my Hidden Heart?

Your Hidden Heart Year Ahead
It is important that you not only reflect on the year that has passed but it is critical that you also feel into your future year ahead. I invite you to gift yourself the time to complete your Heart Existence Mirror and your Future Heart Map and use these to help guide you on your journey towards your Hidden Heart.

YEAR 46 - 54 MARBLES IN YOUR LIFE JAR

Another year of your life has passed, and the hours, days, months, and years of your existence will not be gifted back.

MY HIDDEN HEARTLINES
This is how much time you have already used in your life:

MONTHS	DAYS	HOURS
564	17,155	411,720

This is how much time you have in your life **if** you live to 100:

MONTHS	DAYS	HOURS
648	19,710	473,040

222 *"Be yourself. Everyone else is already taken"*
OSCAR WILDE

"If your dreams don't scare you, they are too small"
SIR RICHARD BRANSON

"Have the courage to follow your heart and intuition, they somehow know what you truly want to become"
STEVE JOBS

YEAR 47 - 53 MARBLES IN YOUR LIFE JAR

Another year of your life has passed, and the hours, days, months, and years of your existence will not be gifted back.

MY HIDDEN HEARTLINES
This is how much time you have already used in your life:

MONTHS	DAYS	HOURS
576	17,520	420,480

This is how much time you have in your life **if** you live to 100:

MONTHS	DAYS	HOURS
636	19,345	464,280

YEAR 48 - 52 MARBLES IN YOUR LIFE JAR

Another year of your life has passed, and the hours, days, months, and years of your existence will not be gifted back.

MY HIDDEN HEARTLINES

This is how much time you have already used in your life:

MONTHS	DAYS	HOURS
588	17,885	429,240

This is how much time you have in your life **if** you live to 100:

MONTHS	DAYS	HOURS
624	18,980	455,520

Your Hidden Heart Diamond

It is time for you to reflect on your life journey this year and truly feel into your heartspace. Have I been connected to Source? Have I been connected to my Inner Child? Have I been connected to my Heart? Have I been connected to my Life Purpose? Have I recognised and been managing my Ego? What is my Hidden Heart?

Your Hidden Heart Year Ahead

It is important that you not only reflect on the year that has passed but it is critical that you also feel into your future year ahead. I invite you to gift yourself the time to complete your Heart Existence Mirror and your Future Heart Map and use these to help guide you on your journey towards your Hidden Heart.

♥ **Author's Heartnote:** It is important to note that when you feel into your heart and reflect over your past seven years there may be significant feelings and emotions that are released, and you need to create a safe space for yourself to heal and grow if this eventuates. If you feel overwhelmed, it is critical that you seek appropriate help and support.

"It is only with the heart that one can see rightly; what is essentially is invisible to the eye"
ANTOINE DE SAINT EXUPERY

"The most beautiful things in the world cannot be seen or even touched they must be felt by the heart"
HELEN KELLER

YOUR SEVEN YEAR HIDDEN HEART LIFE REVIEW

YOUR HIDDEN HEART DIAMOND

How was your connection with Source?

How was your connection with your inner child?

How was your connection with your heart?

How was your connection with your life purpose?

Where was your Ego?

What was your Hidden Heart?

YOUR LIFE JOURNEY

What was your life theme?

What were key heart learnings?

How are you living into my best life now?

What was your greatest achievement from the past seven years? Why do you consider it your greatest achievement?

What was your greatest surprise of the past seven years?

What did you set out to achieve over the past seven years but haven't accomplished it yet?

How will your next seven years be transformative for you?

What do you plan to do to celebrate your beautiful successes over the past seven Years?

What is your legacy gift?

YEAR 49 - 51 MARBLES IN YOUR LIFE JAR

Another year of your life has passed, and the hours, days, months, and years of your existence will not be gifted back.

MY HIDDEN HEARTLINES
This is how much time you have already used in your life:

MONTHS	DAYS	HOURS
600	18,250	438,000

This is how much time you have in your life **if** you live to 100:

MONTHS	DAYS	HOURS
612	18,615	446,760

YEAR 50 - 50 MARBLES IN YOUR LIFE JAR

Another year of your life has passed, and the hours, days, months, and years of your existence will not be gifted back.

MY HIDDEN HEARTLINES
This is how much time you have already used in your life:

MONTHS	DAYS	HOURS
612	18,615	446,760

This is how much time you have in your life **if** you live to 100:

MONTHS	DAYS	HOURS
600	18,250	438,000

Your Hidden Heart Diamond
It is time for you to reflect on your life journey this year and truly feel into your heartspace. Have I been connected to Source? Have I been connected to my Inner Child? Have I been connected to my Heart? Have I been connected to my Life Purpose? Have I recognised and been managing my Ego? What is my Hidden Heart?

Your Hidden Heart Year Ahead
It is important that you not only reflect on the year that has passed but it is critical that you also feel into your future year ahead. I invite you to gift yourself the time to complete your Heart Existence Mirror and your Future Heart Map and use these to help guide you on your journey towards your Hidden Heart.

YEAR 51 - 49 MARBLES IN YOUR LIFE JAR

Another year of your life has passed, and the hours, days, months, and years of your existence will not be gifted back.

MY HIDDEN HEARTLINES
This is how much time you have already used in your life:

MONTHS	DAYS	HOURS
624	18,980	455,520

226 *"Follow your heart and you will never get lost"*
UNKNOWN

This is how much time you have in your life **if** you live to 100:

MONTHS	DAYS	HOURS
588	17,885	429,240

"If you don't follow your heart you might end up spending the rest of your life wishing you had"
UNKNOWN

"Dance with your heart and your feet will follow"
UNKNOWN

"For where your treasure is, there your heart will be also"
MATTHEW 6:21

YEAR 52 - 48 MARBLES IN YOUR LIFE JAR

Another year of your life has passed, and the hours, days, months, and years of your existence will not be gifted back.

MY HIDDEN HEARTLINES
This is how much time you have already used in your life:

MONTHS	DAYS	HOURS
636	19,345	464,280

This is how much time you have in your life **if** you live to 100:

MONTHS	DAYS	HOURS
576	17,520	420,480

YEAR 53 - 47 MARBLES IN YOUR LIFE JAR

Another year of your life has passed, and the hours, days, months, and years of your existence will not be gifted back.

MY HIDDEN HEARTLINES

This is how much time you have already used in your life:

MONTHS	DAYS	HOURS
648	19,710	473,040

This is how much time you have in your life **if** you live to 100:

MONTHS	DAYS	HOURS
564	17,155	411,720

YEAR 54 - 46 MARBLES IN YOUR LIFE JAR

Another year of your life has passed, and the hours, days, months, and years of your existence will not be gifted back.

MY HIDDEN HEARTLINES

This is how much time you have already used in your life:

MONTHS	DAYS	HOURS
660	20,075	481,800

This is how much time you have in your life **if** you live to 100:

MONTHS	DAYS	HOURS
552	116,790	402,960

Your Hidden Heart Diamond 227

It is time for you to reflect on your life journey this year and truly feel into your heartspace. Have I been connected to Source? Have I been connected to my Inner Child? Have I been connected to my Heart? Have I been connected to my Life Purpose? Have I recognised and been managing my Ego? What is my Hidden Heart?

Your Hidden Heart Year Ahead

It is important that you not only reflect on the year that has passed but it is critical that you also feel into your future year ahead. I invite you to gift yourself the time to complete your Heart Existence Mirror and your Future Heart Map and use these to help guide you on your journey towards your Hidden Heart.

YEAR 55 - 45 MARBLES IN YOUR LIFE JAR

Another year of your life has passed, and the hours, days, months, and years of your existence will not be gifted back.

MY HIDDEN HEARTLINES
This is how much time you have already used in your life:

MONTHS	DAYS	HOURS
672	20,440	490,560

This is how much time you have in your life **if** you live to 100:

MONTHS	DAYS	HOURS
540	16,425	394,200

228 *"A beautiful heart can bring things into your life that all the money in the world couldn't buy'"*
UNKNOWN

YOUR SEVEN YEAR HIDDEN HEART LIFE REVIEW

♥ **Author's Heartnote:** It is important to note that when you feel into your heart and reflect over your past seven years there may be significant feelings and emotions that are released, and you need to create a safe space for yourself to heal and grow if this eventuates. If you feel overwhelmed, it is critical that you seek appropriate help and support.

YOUR HIDDEN HEART DIAMOND

How was your connection with Source?

How was your connection with your inner child?

How was your connection with your heart?

How was your connection with your life purpose?

Where was your Ego?

What was your Hidden Heart?

YOUR LIFE JOURNEY

What was your life theme?

What were key heart learnings?

How are you living into my best life now?

What was your greatest achievement from the past seven years? Why do you consider it your greatest achievement?

What was your greatest surprise of the past seven years?

What did you set out to achieve over the past seven years but haven't accomplished it yet?

How will your next seven years be transformative for you?

What do you plan to do to celebrate your beautiful successes over the past seven Years?

What is your legacy gift?

YEAR 56 - 44 MARBLES IN YOUR LIFE JAR

Another year of your life has passed, and the hours, days, months, and years of your existence will not be gifted back.

MY HIDDEN HEARTLINES
This is how much time you have already used in your life:

MONTHS	DAYS	HOURS
684	20,805	499,320

This is how much time you have in your life **if** you live to 100:

MONTHS	DAYS	HOURS
528	16,060	385,440

"By doing what you love, you inspire the hearts of others"
UNKNOWN

"It's not selfish to love yourself and to make your happiness a priority. It's necessary"
UNKNOWN

"To be rich is not what you have in your bank account, but what you have in your heart"
UNKNOWN

"There is an ocean of infinite wisdom in you. Put your hand on your heart and feel it beating"
JENNIFER WILLIAMSON

YEAR 57 - 43 MARBLES IN YOUR LIFE JAR

Another year of your life has passed, and the hours, days, months, and years of your existence will not be gifted back.

MY HIDDEN HEARTLINES
This is how much time you have already used in your life:

MONTHS	DAYS	HOURS
696	21,170	508,080

This is how much time you have in your life **if** you live to 100:

MONTHS	DAYS	HOURS
516	15,695	376,680

YEAR 58 - 42 MARBLES IN YOUR LIFE JAR

Another year of your life has passed, and the hours, days, months, and years of your existence will not be gifted back.

MY HIDDEN HEARTLINES

This is how much time you have already used in your life:

MONTHS	DAYS	HOURS
708	21,535	516,840

This is how much time you have in your life **if** you live to 100:

MONTHS	DAYS	HOURS
504	15,330	367,920

Your Hidden Heart Diamond

231

It is time for you to reflect on your life journey this year and truly feel into your heartspace. Have I been connected to Source? Have I been connected to my Inner Child? Have I been connected to my Heart? Have I been connected to my Life Purpose? Have I recognised and been managing my Ego? What is my Hidden Heart?

Your Hidden Heart Year Ahead

It is important that you not only reflect on the year that has passed but it is critical that you also feel into your future year ahead. I invite you to gift yourself the time to complete your Heart Existence Mirror and your Future Heart Map and use these to help guide you on your journey towards your Hidden Heart.

YEAR 59 - 41 MARBLES IN YOUR LIFE JAR

Another year of your life has passed, and the hours, days, months, and years of your existence will not be gifted back.

MY HIDDEN HEARTLINES

This is how much time you have already used in your life:

MONTHS	DAYS	HOURS
720	21,900	525,600

This is how much time you have in your life **if** you live to 100:

MONTHS	DAYS	HOURS
492	14,965	359,160

YEAR 60 - 40 MARBLES IN YOUR LIFE JAR

Another year of your life has passed, and the hours, days, months, and years of your existence will not be gifted back.

MY HIDDEN HEARTLINES
This is how much time you have already used in your life:

MONTHS	DAYS	HOURS
732	22,265	534,360

This is how much time you have in your life **if** you live to 100:

MONTHS	DAYS	HOURS
480	14,600	350,400

"You change your life by changing your heart"
MAX LUCADO

"Remembering you are going to die is the best way I know to avoid the trap of thinking you have something to lose. You are already naked. There is no reason not to follow your heart"
STEVE JOBS

"Your heart knows things that your mind cannot explain"
UNKNOWN

YEAR 61 - 39 MARBLES IN YOUR LIFE JAR

Another year of your life has passed, and the hours, days, months, and years of your existence will not be gifted back.

MY HIDDEN HEARTLINES
This is how much time you have already used in your life:

MONTHS	DAYS	HOURS
744	22,630	543,120

This is how much time you have in your life **if** you live to 100:

MONTHS	DAYS	HOURS
468	14,235	341,640

YEAR 62 - 38 MARBLES IN YOUR LIFE JAR

Another year of your life has passed, and the hours, days, months, and years of your existence will not be gifted back.

MY HIDDEN HEARTLINES
This is how much time you have already used in your life:

MONTHS	DAYS	HOURS
756	22,995	551,880

This is how much time you have in your life **if** you live to 100:

MONTHS	DAYS	HOURS
456	13,870	332,880

Your Hidden Heart Diamond

It is time for you to reflect on your life journey this year and truly feel into your heartspace. Have I been connected to Source? Have I been connected to my Inner Child? Have I been connected to my Heart? Have I been connected to my Life Purpose? Have I recognised and been managing my Ego? What is my Hidden Heart?

Your Hidden Heart Year Ahead

It is important that you not only reflect on the year that has passed but it is critical that you also feel into your future year ahead. I invite you to gift yourself the time to complete your Heart Existence Mirror and your Future Heart Map and use these to help guide you on your journey towards your Hidden Heart.

♥ **Author's Heartnote:** It is important to note that when you feel into your heart and reflect over your past seven years there may be significant feelings and emotions that are released, and you need to create a safe space for yourself to heal and grow if this eventuates. If you feel overwhelmed, it is critical that you seek appropriate help and support.

"Everything starts and ends with your heart"
DR JOHN MCSWINEY

"Don't be pushed around by the fears in your mind. Be led by the dreams in your heart"
ROY.T. BENNETT

YOUR SEVEN YEAR HIDDEN HEART LIFE REVIEW

YOUR HIDDEN HEART DIAMOND

How was your connection with Source?

How was your connection with your inner child?

How was your connection with your heart?

How was your connection with your life purpose?

Where was your Ego?

What was your Hidden Heart?

YOUR LIFE JOURNEY

What was your life theme?

What were key heart learnings?

How are you living into my best life now?

What was your greatest achievement from the past seven years? Why do you consider it your greatest achievement?

What was your greatest surprise of the past seven years?

What did you set out to achieve over the past seven years but haven't accomplished it yet?

How will your next seven years be transformative for you?

What do you plan to do to celebrate your beautiful successes over the past seven Years?

What is your legacy gift?

YEAR 63 - 37 MARBLES IN YOUR LIFE JAR

Another year of your life has passed, and the hours, days, months, and years of your existence will not be gifted back.

MY HIDDEN HEARTLINES

This is how much time you have already used in your life:

MONTHS	DAYS	HOURS
768	23,360	560,640

This is how much time you have in your life **if** you live to 100:

MONTHS	DAYS	HOURS
444	13,505	324,120

YEAR 64 - 36 MARBLES IN YOUR LIFE JAR

Another year of your life has passed, and the hours, days, months, and years of your existence will not be gifted back.

MY HIDDEN HEARTLINES

This is how much time you have already used in your life:

MONTHS	DAYS	HOURS
780	23,725	569,400

This is how much time you have in your life **if** you live to 100:

MONTHS	DAYS	HOURS
432	13,140	315,360

Your Hidden Heart Diamond   *235*

It is time for you to reflect on your life journey this year and truly feel into your heartspace. Have I been connected to Source? Have I been connected to my Inner Child? Have I been connected to my Heart? Have I been connected to my Life Purpose? Have I recognised and been managing my Ego? What is my Hidden Heart?

Your Hidden Heart Year Ahead

It is important that you not only reflect on the year that has passed but it is critical that you also feel into your future year ahead. I invite you to gift yourself the time to complete your Heart Existence Mirror and your Future Heart Map and use these to help guide you on your journey towards your Hidden Heart.

YEAR 65 - 35 MARBLES IN YOUR LIFE JAR

Another year of your life has passed, and the hours, days, months, and years of your existence will not be gifted back.

MY HIDDEN HEARTLINES
This is how much time you have already used in your life:

MONTHS	DAYS	HOURS
792	24,090	306,600

This is how much time you have in your life **if** you live to 100:

MONTHS	DAYS	HOURS
420	12,775	306,600

"Your toughest challenge will always be between your mind and your heart"
UNKNOWN

"It's impossible, said pride. It's risky, said experience. It's pointless, said reason. Give it a try, said the heart"
UNKNOWN

"Don't let other people chose your path for you. Deep down you know the right way to go, so do the right thing and follow your heart"
UNKNOWN

"It is strange how often a heart must be broken before the years can make it wise"
SARAH TEASDALE

YEAR 66 - 34 MARBLES IN YOUR LIFE JAR

Another year of your life has passed, and the hours, days, months, and years of your existence will not be gifted back.

MY HIDDEN HEARTLINES
This is how much time you have already used in your life:

MONTHS	DAYS	HOURS
804	24,455	586,920

This is how much time you have in your life **if** you live to 100:

MONTHS	DAYS	HOURS
408	12,410	297,840

YEAR 67 - 33 MARBLES IN YOUR LIFE JAR

Another year of your life has passed, and the hours, days, months, and years of your existence will not be gifted back.

MY HIDDEN HEARTLINES
This is how much time you have already used in your life:

MONTHS	DAYS	HOURS
816	24,820	595,680

This is how much time you have in your life **if** you live to 100:

MONTHS	DAYS	HOURS
396	12,045	289,080

YEAR 68 - 32 MARBLES IN YOUR LIFE JAR

Another year of your life has passed, and the hours, days, months, and years of your existence will not be gifted back.

MY HIDDEN HEARTLINES
This is how much time you have already used in your life:

MONTHS	DAYS	HOURS
828	25,185	604,440

This is how much time you have in your life **if** you live to 100:

MONTHS	DAYS	HOURS
384	11,680	280,320

Your Hidden Heart Diamond   *237*

It is time for you to reflect on your life journey this year and truly feel into your heartspace. Have I been connected to Source? Have I been connected to my Inner Child? Have I been connected to my Heart? Have I been connected to my Life Purpose? Have I recognised and been managing my Ego? What is my Hidden Heart?

Your Hidden Heart Year Ahead

It is important that you not only reflect on the year that has passed but it is critical that you also feel into your future year ahead. I invite you to gift yourself the time to complete your Heart Existence Mirror and your Future Heart Map and use these to help guide you on your journey towards your Hidden Heart.

YEAR 69 - 31 MARBLES IN YOUR LIFE JAR

Another year of your life has passed, and the hours, days, months, and years of your existence will not be gifted back.

MY HIDDEN HEARTLINES
This is how much time you have already used in your life:

MONTHS	DAYS	HOURS
840	25,550	613,200

This is how much time you have in your life **if** you live to 100:

MONTHS	DAYS	HOURS
372	11,315	271,560

238

"Be bold enough to use your voice, brave enough to listen to your heart and strong enough to live the life you have always imagined"
UNKNOWN

YOUR SEVEN YEAR HIDDEN HEART LIFE REVIEW

♥ **Author's Heartnote:** It is important to note that when you feel into your heart and reflect over your past seven years there may be significant feelings and emotions that are released, and you need to create a safe space for yourself to heal and grow if this eventuates. If you feel overwhelmed, it is critical that you seek appropriate help and support.

239

YOUR HIDDEN HEART DIAMOND

How was your connection with Source?

How was your connection with your inner child?

How was your connection with your heart?

How was your connection with your life purpose?

Where was your Ego?

What was your Hidden Heart?

YOUR LIFE JOURNEY

What was your life theme?

What were key heart learnings?

How are you living into my best life now?

What was your greatest achievement from the past seven years? Why do you consider it your greatest achievement?

What was your greatest surprise of the past seven years?

What did you set out to achieve over the past seven years but haven't accomplished it yet?

How will your next seven years be transformative for you?

What do you plan to do to celebrate your beautiful successes over the past seven Years?

What is your legacy gift?

YEAR 70 - 30 MARBLES IN YOUR LIFE JAR

Another year of your life has passed, and the hours, days, months, and years of your existence will not be gifted back.

MY HIDDEN HEARTLINES
This is how much time you have already used in your life:

MONTHS	DAYS	HOURS
852	25,915	621,960

This is how much time you have in your life **if** you live to 100:

MONTHS	DAYS	HOURS
360	10,950	262,800

"What you hide in your heart appears in your eyes"
IMAM ALI

"Sometimes the heart should follow the mind. Sometimes the heart should tell the mind to stay at home and stop interfering"
UNKNOWN

"Follow your heart, because if you always trust your mind, you will always act on logic, and logic doesn't always lead to happiness"
UNKNOWN

"You must be the change you want to see in the world"
MAHATMA GHANDI

YEAR 71 - 29 MARBLES IN YOUR LIFE JAR

Another year of your life has passed, and the hours, days, months, and years of your existence will not be gifted back.

MY HIDDEN HEARTLINES
This is how much time you have already used in your life:

MONTHS	DAYS	HOURS
864	26,280	630,720

This is how much time you have in your life **if** you live to 100:

MONTHS	DAYS	HOURS
348	10,585	254,040

YEAR 72 - 28 MARBLES IN YOUR LIFE JAR

Another year of your life has passed, and the hours, days, months, and years of your existence will not be gifted back.

MY HIDDEN HEARTLINES

This is how much time you have already used in your life:

MONTHS	DAYS	HOURS
876	26,645	639,480

This is how much time you have in your life **if** you live to 100:

MONTHS	DAYS	HOURS
336	10,220	245,280

YEAR 73 - 27 MARBLES IN YOUR LIFE JAR

Another year of your life has passed, and the hours, days, months, and years of your existence will not be gifted back.

MY HIDDEN HEARTLINES

This is how much time you have already used in your life:

MONTHS	DAYS	HOURS
888	27,010	648,240

This is how much time you have in your life **if** you live to 100:

MONTHS	DAYS	HOURS
324	9,855	236,520

Your Hidden Heart Diamond *241*

It is time for you to reflect on your life journey this year and truly feel into your heartspace. Have I been connected to Source? Have I been connected to my Inner Child? Have I been connected to my Heart? Have I been connected to my Life Purpose? Have I recognised and been managing my Ego? What is my Hidden Heart?

Your Hidden Heart Year Ahead

It is important that you not only reflect on the year that has passed but it is critical that you also feel into your future year ahead. I invite you to gift yourself the time to complete your Heart Existence Mirror and your Future Heart Map and use these to help guide you on your journey towards your Hidden Heart.

YEAR 74 - 26 MARBLES IN YOUR LIFE JAR

Another year of your life has passed, and the hours, days, months, and years of your existence will not be gifted back.

MY HIDDEN HEARTLINES
This is how much time you have already used in your life:

MONTHS	DAYS	HOURS
900	27,375	657,000

This is how much time you have in your life **if** you live to 100:

MONTHS	DAYS	HOURS
312	9,490	227,760

242

"It is not the length of life but the depth of life"
Ralph Waldo Emerson

"Fill your life with experiences, not things. Have stories to tell, not stuff to show"
UNKNOWN

"Count your age by friends, not years. Count your life by smiles, not tears"
JOHN LENNON

YEAR 75 - 25 MARBLES IN YOUR LIFE JAR

Another year of your life has passed, and the hours, days, months, and years of your existence will not be gifted back.

MY HIDDEN HEARTLINES
This is how much time you have already used in your life:

MONTHS	DAYS	HOURS
912	27,740	665,760

This is how much time you have in your life **if** you live to 100:

MONTHS	DAYS	HOURS
300	9,125	219,000

YEAR 76 - 24 MARBLES IN YOUR LIFE JAR

Another year of your life has passed, and the hours, days, months, and years of your existence will not be gifted back.

MY HIDDEN HEARTLINES
This is how much time you have already used in your life:

MONTHS	DAYS	HOURS
924	28,105	674,520

This is how much time you have in your life **if** you live to 100:

MONTHS	DAYS	HOURS
288	8,760	210,240

Your Hidden Heart Diamond *243*
It is time for you to reflect on your life journey this year and truly feel into your heartspace. Have I been connected to Source? Have I been connected to my Inner Child? Have I been connected to my Heart? Have I been connected to my Life Purpose? Have I recognised and been managing my Ego? What is my Hidden Heart?

Your Hidden Heart Year Ahead
It is important that you not only reflect on the year that has passed but it is critical that you also feel into your future year ahead. I invite you to gift yourself the time to complete your Heart Existence Mirror and your Future Heart Map and use these to help guide you on your journey towards your Hidden Heart.

244 ♥ **Author's Heartnote:** It is important to note that when you feel into your heart and reflect over your past seven years there may be significant feelings and emotions that are released, and you need to create a safe space for yourself to heal and grow if this eventuates. If you feel overwhelmed, it is critical that you seek appropriate help and support.

"The older I get the more I understand that it is ok to live life others don't understand"
UNKNOWN

"Death is not the greatest loss in life. The greatest loss is what dies inside us while we live"
NORMAN COUSINS

YOUR SEVEN YEAR HIDDEN HEART LIFE REVIEW

YOUR HIDDEN HEART DIAMOND

How was your connection with Source?

How was your connection with your inner child?

How was your connection with your heart?

How was your connection with your life purpose?

Where was your Ego?

What was your Hidden Heart?

YOUR LIFE JOURNEY

What was your life theme?

What were key heart learnings?

How are you living into my best life now?

What was your greatest achievement from the past seven years? Why do you consider it your greatest achievement?

What was your greatest surprise of the past seven years?

What did you set out to achieve over the past seven years but haven't accomplished it yet?

How will your next seven years be transformative for you?

What do you plan to do to celebrate your beautiful successes over the past seven Years?

What is your legacy gift?

YEAR 77 - 23 MARBLES IN YOUR LIFE JAR

Another year of your life has passed, and the hours, days, months, and years of your existence will not be gifted back.

MY HIDDEN HEARTLINES
This is how much time you have already used in your life:

MONTHS	DAYS	HOURS
936	28,470	683,280

This is how much time you have in your life **if** you live to 100:

MONTHS	DAYS	HOURS
276	8,395	201,480

YEAR 78 - 22 MARBLES IN YOUR LIFE JAR

Another year of your life has passed, and the hours, days, months, and years of your existence will not be gifted back.

MY HIDDEN HEARTLINES
This is how much time you have already used in your life:

MONTHS	DAYS	HOURS
948	28,835	692,040

This is how much time you have in your life **if** you live to 100:

MONTHS	DAYS	HOURS
264	8,030	192,720

Your Hidden Heart Diamond   *245*
It is time for you to reflect on your life journey this year and truly feel into your heartspace. Have I been connected to Source? Have I been connected to my Inner Child? Have I been connected to my Heart? Have I been connected to my Life Purpose? Have I recognised and been managing my Ego? What is my Hidden Heart?

Your Hidden Heart Year Ahead
It is important that you not only reflect on the year that has passed but it is critical that you also feel into your future year ahead. I invite you to gift yourself the time to complete your Heart Existence Mirror and your Future Heart Map and use these to help guide you on your journey towards your Hidden Heart.

YEAR 79 - 21 MARBLES IN YOUR LIFE JAR

Another year of your life has passed, and the hours, days, months, and years of your existence will not be gifted back.

MY HIDDEN HEARTLINES
This is how much time you have already used in your life:

MONTHS	DAYS	HOURS
960	29,200	700,800

This is how much time you have in your life **if** you live to 100:

MONTHS	DAYS	HOURS
252	7,665	183,960

"Accept no-one's definition of your life; define yourself"
UNKNOWN

"You are never too old to set another goal or to dream a new dream"
UNKNOWN

"We have two lives: the one we learn with and the life we live after that"
BERNARD MALMUD

"Never regret a day in your life. Good days give you happiness and bad days give you experience"
UNKNOWN

YEAR 80 - 20 MARBLES IN YOUR LIFE JAR

Another year of your life has passed, and the hours, days, months, and years of your existence will not be gifted back.

MY HIDDEN HEARTLINES
This is how much time you have already used in your life:

MONTHS	DAYS	HOURS
972	29,565	709,560

This is how much time you have in your life **if** you live to 100:

MONTHS	DAYS	HOURS
240	7,300	175,200

YEAR 81 - 19 MARBLES IN YOUR LIFE JAR

Another year of your life has passed, and the hours, days, months, and years of your existence will not be gifted back.

MY HIDDEN HEARTLINES

This is how much time you have already used in your life:

MONTHS	DAYS	HOURS
984	29,930	718,320

This is how much time you have in your life **if** you live to 100:

MONTHS	DAYS	HOURS
228	6,935	166,440

YEAR 82 - 18 MARBLES IN YOUR LIFE JAR

Another year of your life has passed, and the hours, days, months, and years of your existence will not be gifted back.

MY HIDDEN HEARTLINES

This is how much time you have already used in your life:

MONTHS	DAYS	HOURS
996	30,295	727,080

This is how much time you have in your life **if** you live to 100:

MONTHS	DAYS	HOURS
216	6,570	157,680

Your Hidden Heart Diamond   *247*

It is time for you to reflect on your life journey this year and truly feel into your heartspace. Have I been connected to Source? Have I been connected to my Inner Child? Have I been connected to my Heart? Have I been connected to my Life Purpose? Have I recognised and been managing my Ego? What is my Hidden Heart?

Your Hidden Heart Year Ahead

It is important that you not only reflect on the year that has passed but it is critical that you also feel into your future year ahead. I invite you to gift yourself the time to complete your Heart Existence Mirror and your Future Heart Map and use these to help guide you on your journey towards your Hidden Heart.

YEAR 83 - 17 MARBLES IN YOUR LIFE JAR

Another year of your life has passed, and the hours, days, months, and years of your existence will not be gifted back.

MY HIDDEN HEARTLINES
This is how much time you have already used in your life:

MONTHS	DAYS	HOURS
1008	30,660	735,840

This is how much time you have in your life **if** you live to 100:

MONTHS	DAYS	HOURS
204	6,205	148,920

248

"Once your life is an expression of your blissfulness, you will not be in conflict with anyone"
SADHGURU

YOUR SEVEN YEAR HIDDEN HEART LIFE REVIEW

YOUR HIDDEN HEART DIAMOND

How was your connection with Source?

How was your connection with your inner child?

How was your connection with your heart?

How was your connection with your life purpose?

Where was your Ego?

What was your Hidden Heart?

YOUR LIFE JOURNEY

What was your life theme?

What were key heart learnings?

How are you living into my best life now?

What was your greatest achievement from the past seven years? Why do you consider it your greatest achievement?

What was your greatest surprise of the past seven years?

What did you set out to achieve over the past seven years but haven't accomplished it yet?

How will your next seven years be transformative for you?

What do you plan to do to celebrate your beautiful successes over the past seven Years?

What is your legacy gift?

♥ **Author's Heartnote:** It is *249* important to note that when you feel into your heart and reflect over your past seven years there may be significant feelings and emotions that are released, and you need to create a safe space for yourself to heal and grow if this eventuates. If you feel overwhelmed, it is critical that you seek appropriate help and support.

YEAR 84 - 16 MARBLES IN YOUR LIFE JAR

Another year of your life has passed, and the hours, days, months, and years of your existence will not be gifted back.

MY HIDDEN HEARTLINES
This is how much time you have already used in your life:

MONTHS	DAYS	HOURS
1,020	31,025	744,600

"Never let the sadness of your past and the fear of the future upset the happiness of your present"
UNKNOWN

"Living your best life is your most important journey in life"
OPRAH WINFREY

"Life is the greatest journey you will ever be on"
UNKNOWN

"Happiness is not something you postpone for the future; it is something you design for the present"
JIM ROHN

This is how much time you have in your life **if** you live to 100:

MONTHS	DAYS	HOURS
192	5,840	140,160

YEAR 85 - 15 MARBLES IN YOUR LIFE JAR

Another year of your life has passed, and the hours, days, months, and years of your existence will not be gifted back.

MY HIDDEN HEARTLINES
This is how much time you have already used in your life:

MONTHS	DAYS	HOURS
1,032	31,390	753,360

This is how much time you have in your life **if** you live to 100:

MONTHS	DAYS	HOURS
180	5,475	131,400

YEAR 86 - 14 MARBLES IN YOUR LIFE JAR

Another year of your life has passed, and the hours, days, months, and years of your existence will not be gifted back.

MY HIDDEN HEARTLINES
This is how much time you have already used in your life:

MONTHS	DAYS	HOURS
1,044	31,755	762,120

This is how much time you have in your life **if** you live to 100:

MONTHS	DAYS	HOURS
168	5,110	122,640

YEAR 87 - 13 MARBLES IN YOUR LIFE JAR

Another year of your life has passed, and the hours, days, months, and years of your existence will not be gifted back.

MY HIDDEN HEARTLINES
This is how much time you have already used in your life:

MONTHS	DAYS	HOURS
1,056	32,120	770,880

This is how much time you have in your life **if** you live to 100:

MONTHS	DAYS	HOURS
156	4,745	113,880

251

Your Hidden Heart Diamond
It is time for you to reflect on your life journey this year and truly feel into your heartspace. Have I been connected to Source? Have I been connected to my Inner Child? Have I been connected to my Heart? Have I been connected to my Life Purpose? Have I recognised and been managing my Ego? What is my Hidden Heart?

Your Hidden Heart Year Ahead
It is important that you not only reflect on the year that has passed but it is critical that you also feel into your future year ahead. I invite you to gift yourself the time to complete your Heart Existence Mirror and your Future Heart Map and use these to help guide you on your journey towards your Hidden Heart.

YEAR 88 - 12 MARBLES IN YOUR LIFE JAR

Another year of your life has passed, and the hours, days, months, and years of your existence will not be gifted back.

MY HIDDEN HEARTLINES
This is how much time you have already used in your life:

MONTHS	DAYS	HOURS
1,068	32,485	779,640

This is how much time you have in your life **if** you live to 100:

MONTHS	DAYS	HOURS
144	4,380	105,120

"In three words I can sum up every-thing I have learned about life: it goes on"
ROBERT FROST

"The meaning of life is to find your gift. The purpose of life is to give it away"
WILLIAM SHAKESPEARE

"Love people, use things. The oppo-site never works"
THE MINIMALISTS

YEAR 89 - 11 MARBLES IN YOUR LIFE JAR

Another year of your life has passed, and the hours, days, months, and years of your existence will not be gifted back.

MY HIDDEN HEARTLINES
This is how much time you have already used in your life:

MONTHS	DAYS	HOURS
1,080	32,850	788,400

This is how much time you have in your life **if** you live to 100:

MONTHS	DAYS	HOURS
132	4,015	96,360

YEAR 90 - 10 MARBLES IN YOUR LIFE JAR

Another year of your life has passed, and the hours, days, months, and years of your existence will not be gifted back.

MY HIDDEN HEARTLINES
This is how much time you have already used in your life:

MONTHS	DAYS	HOURS
1,092	33,215	797,160

This is how much time you have in your life **if** you live to 100

MONTHS	DAYS	HOURS
120	3,650	87,600

Your Hidden Heart Diamond   *253*

It is time for you to reflect on your life journey this year and truly feel into your heartspace. Have I been connected to Source? Have I been connected to my Inner Child? Have I been connected to my Heart? Have I been connected to my Life Purpose? Have I recognised and been managing my Ego? What is my Hidden Heart?

Your Hidden Heart Year Ahead

It is important that you not only reflect on the year that has passed but it is critical that you also feel into your future year ahead. I invite you to gift yourself the time to complete your Heart Existence Mirror and your Future Heart Map and use these to help guide you on your journey towards your Hidden Heart.

254 ♥ **Author's Heartnote:** It is important to note that when you feel into your heart and reflect over your past seven years there may be significant feelings and emotions that are released, and you need to create a safe space for yourself to heal and grow if this eventuates. If you feel overwhelmed, it is critical that you seek appropriate help and support.

"If you can do best and be happy, you are further along in life than most people"
LEONARDO DI CAPRIO

"We are all visitors to this time, this place. We are just passing through. Our purpose here is to learn, to grow, to love ... And then we return home"
UNKNOWN

YOUR SEVEN YEAR HIDDEN HEART LIFE REVIEW

YOUR HIDDEN HEART DIAMOND

How was your connection with Source?

How was your connection with your inner child?

How was your connection with your heart?

How was your connection with your life purpose?

Where was your Ego?

What was your Hidden Heart?

YOUR LIFE JOURNEY

What was your life theme?

What were key heart learnings?

How are you living into my best life now?

What was your greatest achievement from the past seven years? Why do you consider it your greatest achievement?

What was your greatest surprise of the past seven years?

What did you set out to achieve over the past seven years but haven't accomplished it yet?

How will your next seven years be transformative for you?

What do you plan to do to celebrate your beautiful successes over the past seven Years?

What is your legacy gift?

YEAR 91 - 9 MARBLES IN YOUR LIFE JAR

Another year of your life has passed, and the hours, days, months, and years of your existence will not be gifted back.

MY HIDDEN HEARTLINES

This is how much time you have already used in your life:

MONTHS	DAYS	HOURS
1,104	33,580	805,920

This is how much time you have in your life **if** you live to 100:

MONTHS	DAYS	HOURS
108	3,285	78,840

YEAR 92 - 8 MARBLES IN YOUR LIFE JAR

Another year of your life has passed, and the hours, days, months, and years of your existence will not be gifted back.

MY HIDDEN HEARTLINES

This is how much time you have already used in your life:

MONTHS	DAYS	HOURS
1,116	33,945	814,680

This is how much time you have in your life **if** you live to 100:

MONTHS	DAYS	HOURS
96	2,920	70,080

Your Hidden Heart Diamond

It is time for you to reflect on your life journey this year and truly feel into your heartspace. Have I been connected to Source? Have I been connected to my Inner Child? Have I been connected to my Heart? Have I been connected to my Life Purpose? Have I recognised and been managing my Ego? What is my Hidden Heart?

Your Hidden Heart Year Ahead

It is important that you not only reflect on the year that has passed but it is critical that you also feel into your future year ahead. I invite you to gift yourself the time to complete your Heart Existence Mirror and your Future Heart Map and use these to help guide you on your journey towards your Hidden Heart.

YEAR 93 - 7 MARBLES IN YOUR LIFE JAR

Another year of your life has passed, and the hours, days, months, and years of your existence will not be gifted back.

MY HIDDEN HEARTLINES
This is how much time you have already used in your life:

MONTHS	DAYS	HOURS
1,128	34,310	823,330

This is how much time you have in your life **if** you live to 100:

MONTHS	DAYS	HOURS
84	2,555	61,320

"When life is good you are happy. When you are happy life is good. Knowing the difference is the key"
UNKNOWN

"When life is sweet say thank you and celebrate. When life is bitter, say thank you and grow"
UNKNOWN

"Life always offers you a second chance, it's called tomorrow"
UNKNOWN

"No-one on his deathbed said, 'I wish I had of spent more time at the office"
PAUL TSONGAS

YEAR 94 - 6 MARBLES IN YOUR LIFE JAR

Another year of your life has passed, and the hours, days, months, and years of your existence will not be gifted back.

MY HIDDEN HEARTLINES
This is how much time you have already used in your life:

MONTHS	DAYS	HOURS
1,140	34,675	832,200

This is how much time you have in your life **if** you live to 100:

MONTHS	DAYS	HOURS
72	2,190	52,560

YEAR 95 - 5 MARBLES IN YOUR LIFE JAR

Another year of your life has passed, and the hours, days, months, and years of your existence will not be gifted back.

MY HIDDEN HEARTLINES
This is how much time you have already used in your life:

MONTHS	DAYS	HOURS
1,152	35,040	840,960

This is how much time you have in your life **if** you live to 100:

MONTHS	DAYS	HOURS
60	1,825	43,800

YEAR 96 - 4 MARBLES IN YOUR LIFE JAR

Another year of your life has passed, and the hours, days, months, and years of your existence will not be gifted back.

MY HIDDEN HEARTLINES
This is how much time you have already used in your life:

MONTHS	DAYS	HOURS
1,152	35,405	849,720

This is how much time you have in your life **if** you live to 100:

MONTHS	DAYS	HOURS
48	1,460	35,040

Your Hidden Heart Diamond   *257*
It is time for you to reflect on your life journey this year and truly feel into your heartspace. Have I been connected to Source? Have I been connected to my Inner Child? Have I been connected to my Heart? Have I been connected to my Life Purpose? Have I recognised and been managing my Ego? What is my Hidden Heart?

Your Hidden Heart Year Ahead
It is important that you not only reflect on the year that has passed but it is critical that you also feel into your future year ahead. I invite you to gift yourself the time to complete your Heart Existence Mirror and your Future Heart Map and use these to help guide you on your journey towards your Hidden Heart.

YEAR 97 - 3 MARBLES IN YOUR LIFE JAR

Another year of your life has passed, and the hours, days, months, and years of your existence will not be gifted back.

MY HIDDEN HEARTLINES

This is how much time you have already used in your life:

MONTHS	DAYS	HOURS
1,164	35,770	858,480

This is how much time you have in your life **if** you live to 100:

MONTHS	DAYS	HOURS
36	1,095	26,280

"In the end, it's not the years in your life that count. It's the life in your years"
ABRAHAM LINCOLN

YOUR SEVEN YEAR HIDDEN HEART LIFE REVIEW

YOUR HIDDEN HEART DIAMOND

How was your connection with Source?

How was your connection with your inner child?

How was your connection with your heart?

How was your connection with your life purpose?

Where was your Ego?

What was your Hidden Heart?

YOUR LIFE JOURNEY

What was your life theme?

What were key heart learnings?

How are you living into my best life now?

What was your greatest achievement from the past seven years? Why do you consider it your greatest achievement?

What was your greatest surprise of the past seven years?

What did you set out to achieve over the past seven years but haven't accomplished it yet?

How will your next seven years be transformative for you?

What do you plan to do to celebrate your beautiful successes over the past seven Years?

What is your legacy gift?

♥ **Author's Heartnote:** It is *259* important to note that when you feel into your heart and reflect over your past seven years there may be significant feelings and emotions that are released, and you need to create a safe space for yourself to heal and grow if this eventuates. If you feel overwhelmed, it is critical that you seek appropriate help and support.

YEAR 98 - 2 MARBLES IN YOUR LIFE JAR

Another year of your life has passed, and the hours, days, months, and years of your existence will not be gifted back.

MY HIDDEN HEARTLINES
This is how much time you have already used in your life:

MONTHS	DAYS	HOURS
1,176	36,135	867,240

This is how much time you have in your life **if** you live to 100:

MONTHS	DAYS	HOURS
24	730	17,520

"One day your life will flash before your eyes. Make sure it's worth watching"
ABRAHAM LINCOLN

"The only thing permanent in this life is that everything is temporary"
UNKNOWN

"Life is what you celebrate. All of it. Even its end"
UNKNOWN

YEAR 99 - 1 MARBLE IN YOUR LIFE JAR

Another year of your life has passed, and the hours, days, months, and years of your existence will not be gifted back.

MY HIDDEN HEARTLINES
This is how much time you have already used in your life:

MONTHS	DAYS	HOURS
1,188	36,500	876,000

This is how much time you have in your life **if** you live to 100:

MONTHS	DAYS	HOURS
12	365	8,760

YEAR 100 - 0 MARBLES IN YOUR LIFE JAR

Another year of your life has passed, and the hours, days, months, and years of your existence will not be gifted back.

MY HIDDEN HEARTLINES

This is how much time you have already used in your life:

MONTHS	DAYS	HOURS
1,200	36,500	876,000

This is how much time you have in your life **if** you live to 100:

MONTHS	DAYS	HOURS
0	0	0

CONGRATULATIONS ON YOUR 100TH HIDDEN HEART YEAR

Your Hidden Heart Diamond *261*

It is time for you to reflect on your life journey this year and truly feel into your heartspace. Have I been connected to Source? Have I been connected to my Inner Child? Have I been connected to my Heart? Have I been connected to my Life Purpose? Have I recognised and been managing my Ego? What is my Hidden Heart?

Your Hidden Heart Year Ahead

It is important that you not only reflect on the year that has passed but it is critical that you also feel into your future year ahead. I invite you to gift yourself the time to complete your Heart Existence Mirror and your Future Heart Map and use these to help guide you on your journey towards your Hidden Heart.

APPENDIX

ACKNOWLEDGEMENTS

As I sit here and feel into writing the acknowledgement section of this Book, it will be impossible to formally acknowledge every person who has contributed to my life journey.

This Book is a lifetime work created over twenty years that was composed by a myriad of souls and I am but the writer weaving all the invisible strands together.

I am eternally indebted to every soul that has interacted with me and enabled me to become the person I am today. Every interaction, whether positive or negative was a life lesson that brought me closer to my own heart and gifted me with the opportunity to discover my own Hidden Heart.

I would like to start by offering a beautiful heartfelt thankyou to you for having the courage to choose to believe in yourself and travel inwards to discover who you were truly meant to be. The most fulfilling relationship is the one that you have with Self and the most beautiful journey you will ever embark on is the one that connects You with your heart so step up and live into it.

To my mother and father Joan and Terry McSwiney without whom I would not be here. Life was not always easy, but it was a beautiful journey, and I was blessed to have two unique souls as my parents. I would not be the man I am today without their love, support, encouragement, and commitment to provide me with a better life than what they experienced. I will forever be indebted to them, and I love them both dearly.

To my brother Daniel McSwiney who I shared a great life with, for his first 20 years up until a fateful night on 5 August 1989 when he was killed by a drunk driver. We travelled together, played football together, went to school together, surfed together and shared a lifetime worth of precious memories. Daniel was full of life and joy. He lived to surf and his passion was infectious. A truly beautiful soul who was taken far too soon. I learnt much from you in life and even more since you passed, especially about forgiveness, self-compassion, and healing.

To my sister Jayne McSwiney, a great artist, creative art director and direct voice channel. We have journeyed together our whole lives and experienced much, even for just one life-time. It has certainly been interesting.

To my three magnificent children Ryan, Connor and Elle McSwiney, words cannot express how much I love you and how proud I am of each of you. When I wrote The Marble Book Ryan and Connor were only babies lol It has been a privilege to have a front row seat to watch you all grow into beautiful young adults and I have learnt a lot about love and compassion by being your Dad. You inspire me; I love the way we all love each other and can express our love openly and from our hearts. Thank you for being who you are.

To Robyn Hayes who is a lovely soul, and we were married for 14 years and had three beautiful children together. Robyn is a beautiful soul with a massive heart for others and has been a good friend for over twenty years. I have been blessed to have her in my life.

To all my family and friends in Australia, Derry, Northern Ireland, Scotland, and the United States of America. I have been blessed with an extended Celtic family and am very proud of my roots, my heritage, and my clan. It has been a lively journey that has taught me much.

To all the souls who I worked and journeyed with in the Australian Labor Party, Monash University, the University of Tasmania, Deakin University, Taylor Splatt and Partners Lawyers, The Legal Ombudsman, The Equal Opportunity Commission, the Victorian Government, The Department of Education, the Victorian Curriculum and Assessment Authority, Haileybury College and the Haileybury International School, China, and The Royal Australian Navy. Thank you for showing me and teaching me many valuable life lessons.

To all my friends in surf lifesaving and the beautiful souls at Chelsea Longbeach Surf Lifesaving Club and the Bonbeach Lifesaving Club where I have spent many fun years patrolling the beaches and laughing and having fun with beautiful people who have great hearts for community service. Thank you for keeping my heart open for joy, fun and being a conduit for my inner child to come out and go crazy!

**I AM ETERNALLY GRATEFUL
FOR ALL OF YOU XX**

ABOUT THE AUTHOR

Dr John McSwiney is a neuroscience based coach and author. He journeys with people all over the world to help them connect with their hearts and live their best lives. He is a passionate about his three children and he lives for the water and loves surfing, SUPing, open water swimming and surf lifesaving.

Dr John has spent his professional career searching for ways to advance and improve the world in which he has found himself. He has had careers in politics, law, government, education, defence and international business. He has spent over 20 years working in senior executive and C-suite roles across government and the private sector both in Australia and internationally.

Dr John possesses a wealth of knowledge and experience working closely with individuals, groups and teams. His neuroscience based coaching is designed to empower you from your heart to live a life true to yourself, and not the life others expect of you. He utilises mBraining neurological techniques together with NLP frameworks and matrix and timeline therapies to achieve life changing outcomes. He has degrees in Social Science, Law and a Master of Arts and PhD in Philosophy from Monash University.

Dr John was admitted as a Barrister and Solicitor of the Supreme Court of Victoria in April 1999. He is a certified mBIT Practitioner, Practitioner of Neuro Linguistic Programming (NLP), Timline (Matrix) Practitioner and a Conscious Hypnosis Practitioner.

EMERGENCY HELPLINES

Your Hidden Heart journey is an intensely personal one that can affect you at a deep level. It is important that in the event you are feeling overwhelmed or need assistance that you reach out for help.

Your life's journey is to go inward, heal and grow and sometimes you need to journey with others who can help you achieve this. There is no shame in this, and it is a sign of strength and growth to reach out, so if you need to, find your courage and do it.

I have included a few organisations for you to consider depending on your own unique circumstances:

AUSTRALIA
- Lifeline - 1311414; www.lifeline.org.au
- Lifeline provide 24/7 crisis support and assistance.
- Beyond Blue – 1300224636; www.beyondblue.org.au
- Beyond Blue provide 24/7 mental health support and assistance.
- Friendline – www.friendline.org.au
- Friendline is for anyone who needs to reconnect or just wants to chat.

CANADA

- Wellness Together CA – 1-866-585-0445; www.wellnesstogether.ca
- Wellness Together CA is a 24/7 support service focusing on wellness and emotional support.

NEW ZEALAND

- Lifeline – 0800543354 (0800 Lifeline) www.lifeline.org.nz
- Lifeline Aotearoa's is a 24/7 community support and helpline
- Samaritans – 0800726666; www.samaritans.org.nz
- Samaritans provide 24/7 support if you are experiencing loneliness, depression, despair, distress, or suicidal feelings.

UK

- Samaritans – 116123; www.samaritans.org
- Samaritans provide 24/7 support to make sure there is always someone there for anyone who needs someone.
- Supportline – 01708765200; www.supportline.org.uk
- SupportLine provides a confidential telephone helpline offering emotional support to any individual on any issue.

USA

- Crisis Text Line – Text HOME to 741741; www.samaritanshope.org
- Crisis Text Line provides free, 24/7, high-quality text-based mental health support and crisis intervention.
- Samaritans Hope – (877)8704673; www.samaritanshope.org
- Samaritans Hope provide 24/7 support if you are experiencing loneliness, depression, despair, distress, or suicidal feelings.